Mascot Books
560 Herndon Parkway #120
Herndon, VA 20170
info@mascotbooks.com

PRW0514A

Library of Congress Control Number: 2014930054

ISBN-10: 1620864959
ISBN-13: 9781620864951

Printed in the United States

www.mascotbooks.com

Every Day is Sweeter

From Widowed to Bliss - Trace the Thread

k Crownover Ron Gillespie

WE DEDICATE THIS BOOK TO
PEOPLE WHO DREAM OF AN END
BETTER THAN THE BEGINNING!

"So the Lord blessed the latter end of
Job more than his beginning..."
Job 42:12

Ronlovesk@yahoo.com

Acknowledgments

Thanks for your encouragement and interest...

Barbara Ball

Rebecca Crownover

Stephanie & Justin Crownover

Janice Fulce

Greg Goodrich

Russ Goodrich

Rochelle Hutcherson

Darla Leggett

Sheri Mager

Jagee & Larry Dan Melton

Lisa Mitchell

Melanie Pouncey

Johnye Sharp

Geneva Towndrow

Jennifer Williams

Karen Williams

Laura Vasile, my project manager, for her tireless efforts
to give me exactly the book I envisioned.

Life Gets Better

After the death of our spouses, Ron and I often felt life was over. It was as if we were merely waiting to join Betty and John in heaven. We didn't feel that way all the time, but we felt it far too often. Since the day we met and made that simple confession to one another, life has turned around. Those feelings were the first thing we had in common, but they certainly were not the last. Before we met, our lives could not have been more different, but we brought them together to form the best of our story.

We love to tell our amazing story in person and watch the expressions on people's faces. But just in case we don't run into you, we thought we should write it down so everyone could enjoy it.

Ron was with Betty for 39 years, and I was with John for 36. Our marriages weren't perfect, but we considered them well above average. We never dreamed that someday we'd have a late-in-life marriage that could hold a candle to what we'd lost. When we found ourselves single again, our biggest fear was that people our age were all grumpy, old fuddy-duddies set in their ways and impossible to please. We'd heard, "You can't teach an old dog new tricks, and a leopard can't change its spots!" That was wrong. It can be done. WE KNOW BECAUSE **SOMEHOW** WE DID IT!

We never had a plan to write a book or to build a marriage that was anything other than typical. Without big dreams or making grand promises to one another, we simply headed out. What a shock! We thought we bought tickets for the bus but they turned out to be for a hot air balloon instead. Our story tells how we stumbled upon a marriage unlike anything we had ever known before. We hadn't seen it in our parents' marriages or our previous marriages.

Our story is the whole truth, and nothing but the truth. Our friends and families may be a little shocked, but this is the way it really happened. We will not blame, protect, brag, or whine. So come with us, and we'll start at the very beginning. You'll see how totally opposite our younger years were, meet our folks, go to school, peek in at the wedding, take a quick glance at a few of our unforgettable memories from previous marriages, and learn how we felt when Betty got sick and John had his accident. We stagger. We fall down, dazed. But eventually we get back on our feet and discover there is life after death for the spouse who *survives*.

I'm going to do most of the writing, but I convinced Ron to also tell his side of the story because women like to know what men really think. It's only fair that the weight of the writing should rest on my shoulders because, after all, writing our story has been my dream, not his. So, ladies, I'll share a little bit of my wonderful husband's life with you, and we hope you'll enjoy it.

Little Pieces
of Childhood Memories

Moving on up to the West Side

I was born February 23, 1943 in Pampa, Texas, to Elvan and Lois Marie Gillespie. I had 2 older sisters, Leticia and Gloria, a younger brother, Taylor, and my 2 youngest sisters, Debbie and Donna.

It was an exciting day when my parents moved our family of 7 (it was shortly before Donna was born) from a small 2-bedroom house on North Mars Street to Sunset Terrace in the Country Club Addition. I was 11 at the time. North Mars was a dirt street, and I couldn't believe Sunset Terrace was paved. Our new living room had a tiny gas fireplace with electric sconces on the sides and candelabra light bulbs. It felt like a palace! We'd increased to 3 bedrooms, but we still had only one bathroom. My parents put Taylor and me in the detached garage on bunk beds. The garage had no insulation in the walls, no heat, and no running water. Our private bathroom was the tree outside our window. We were 9 and 11 years old, and it was little boy heaven to us! All our friends envied us, and they were always anxious to spend the night. I told Taylor we needed to remember to complain as if we hated it or our folks might make us move into the house with them someday. So we complained, and it worked. I didn't move out of our one-car garage apartment until I went off to college.

Mother had her eye on a better life for her children. She enrolled us in formal dance lessons and outfitted us for the Sarbanes and Cotillion dances. I got to play Kids Incorporated softball and football. Mom sent me to apply for the sack boy job at the grocery store. She gave Taylor and me a dime for the offering at church, and we walked to Sunday school.

We were among the first families on the block to get a little, round, black and white TV set. All summer we played neighborhood games in the evening except for the night *I Love Lucy* came on. Then, 25 to 30 kids crammed inside our living room to watch *Lucy*.

Only 3 blocks away in Sam Houston Park was the city recreational shed where we were allowed to check out games and balls. The park was on a slope that ran down to a huge stage where they put on band concerts and plays. Everything was free; all we needed was our blanket to sit on. I still remember seeing a play about Tom Sawyer and Huckleberry Finn painting a fence. For just a nickel, we could buy snow cones from Sno-Joe, a college boy who sold snow cones in our neighborhood all summer long. But the best summer treat of all was going to the swimming pool when we had enough money.

After all their children left home, my parents decided to move. They put a "For Sale" sign in their front yard. Several of the neighbors got together, pulled up the sign, knocked on the front door, handed my parents the sign, and said, "Here's your sign. We're not letting you move out of our neighborhood."

My dad was so touched that he said to my mother, "Well, Momma, I guess we're staying," and they stayed in that same little house for the rest of their lives.

She Was My Real Hero 😊

Until we moved across town when I was in the fourth grade, my only outstanding memory was when Georgie Becky stole my stick horse, and our mothers got into an argument about it.

Mrs. Becky told my mother, "It's a good thing for you that you're pregnant."

My mom said, "Don't let that stop you!" as she peeled off her sweater, threw it on the ground, and started up their front porch steps.

Mrs. Becky locked herself in the house with Georgie. Soon their front door opened just a crack, and my stick horse was tossed out into the yard. I LOVED MY MOM!

Pals 😊

Growing up, my best buddy was Eddie Lester. I still remember when my family was sitting at a red light, and a wrecker drove in front of us pulling a wrecked car. My mom gasped and commented that whoever was in that car wreck surely didn't survive. When we got home we learned that the teenagers who had died in that car crash were Eddie's big sister, Beverly, and her boyfriend. Eddie's family was so torn up, especially his dad, that they soon moved away. It was a sad time for me and all the kids in my neighborhood.

I'll always remember when Limon Stubblefield and Jim Wade Baker, older neighborhood boys, invited me to campout on the prairie with them. We took bottled Cokes and tied a string around their necks to lower them to the bottom of the creek where the water was the coldest. We made a campfire, ate sandwiches we'd made at home, and drank our ice-cold Cokes. Later we roasted marshmallows, told ghost stories, and slept out under the stars. The next morning it was a little scary when 3 horsemen rode up. They questioned us sternly, and then told us to make sure our campfire was completely out before we left. My friends assured them they knew about safety because they were boy scouts. Limon and Jim Wade invited me to join the scouts when I was 11, and I stayed involved even after they dropped out.

I had many good friends and just as many good experiences in scouts, working, and playing sports. My childhood was full of wonderful memories, and there's little I would change even if I could.

Silence Isn't Always the Best Policy

My mom was a strong woman and a great mother. My dad tried to affectionately call her Momma, but she didn't like it. She felt her 6 children called her that quite enough. Maybe my dad would have preferred to be one of the kids instead of her husband when she was on the war path. She didn't have much patience with him.

As a teenager, I noticed when my parents weren't getting along my dad just left the house for hours. When he returned, nothing was ever said. I remember he moved out when I was pretty little, but he eventually moved back in. As an adult, he told me many times that he came back for the sake of his children. If my dad moved back home to my mom without a word of explanation or ever settling their differences, that would explain a lot about my mother and why she had unresolved anger.

I Couldn't Please Them Both

I grew much faster than my siblings. When I was 13 and Taylor was 11, we were fairly close to the same size. But by the time I was 15, there was such a difference in our size that I could have practically passed for his dad. Because I was a big guy, upper classmen frequently challenged me. My mom was my mainstay. She told me, "Don't ever start a fight, but always defend yourself. I expect you to finish anything that gets started."

When Mom was young, her mother told her she would be punished if she stood by and watched her brothers get beaten in a fight without helping them.

My dad's childhood was just the opposite. He went to a one-room school with his siblings, and he was the youngest student. In all of his lectures about not fighting, he never told of a single instance when he'd been challenged and walked away. He didn't take that into account when he boasted that he'd never been in a fight. He didn't avoid fights, they just didn't come his way.

With my dad ordering me not to fight and threatening to punish me if I did, and my mom taking me aside and telling me to always stand my ground and defend myself, I was in a no-win situation. Their mixed messages forced me to make the decision for myself since I obviously couldn't please them both. I decided I'd rather stand up for myself and be punished by my dad. I never enjoyed fighting. I never started a fight. Even though I tried to avoid fights, it never worked! When guys decided they wanted to fight me, there was no talking them out of it.

True to his word, my dad punished me for fighting. He took away my driver's license, made me put my car up on cinder blocks, pull the wheels off, and store them in the garage. To impress me further, he held up a 16-pound sledge hammer and said if he caught me putting the wheels back on my car and driving, he'd take that hammer and beat my car into a worthless piece of metal.

Permanently Impressed at 10

My dad's greatest fear was that I would grow up to be like my mother's younger brother, Warren. He and I were both strong and playful. We both loved little kids and they were always naturally drawn to us, but Uncle Warren was a drinker and a fighter. More than once he became so unruly that my grandmother was forced to call the sheriff. The sheriff would call in all the off duty officers for additional help. It took all of them to chain my Uncle Warren to the tree in my grandmother's front yard where he couldn't cause any more trouble until he sobered up.

My dad liked to say, about my mother's side of the family, "They were the family that should have never been."

He was determined that he would prevent me from becoming like my Uncle Warren. He really didn't have anything to worry about. I learned to fight because I had no choice, but I never liked it. And when I drank, it was always in moderation because of Warren's example.

Of my many uncles, Warren was the favorite of all the nieces and nephews but only when he was *sober*. His alcoholism saved me as a young man because it taught me to be extremely cautious when it came to drinking. My Uncle Warren actually became the most beneficial example in my life of what **not** to do.

I was only 10 the day we went to my grandmother's house and what I saw changed my life. When we pulled up, Uncle Warren was out in the yard, lying in the sun during the hottest part of the day. As we went in the house, I could see the whole front of his pants were wet.

Out of concern I asked Uncle Lowell, "What's wrong with Uncle Warren?"

He told me, "You just stay away from him and let him sober up. He's *mean* when he's drunk. You leave him alone."

That horrible memory never left me. The fact that he stole his mother's social security checks, spent time in prison, and drank everything in the cabinets, including bleach, did not impress me at 10 years of age as much as wetting his pants. I suppose what will most impact a child is unpredictable. Uncle Warren's example prevented me from drinking too much and from experimenting with drugs when I moved to southern California as a young man in the 60s.

Shouldering Responsibility

My dad had an opportunity to go into business for himself as a milk distributor. It was his lifelong dream to own and operate a family business that he could eventually hand down to his sons. I was only 14 when my dad collapsed at the dinner table. The doctors told him he had a heart attack, and if he wanted to survive, he must never exert himself again. He followed the doctor's orders, but in the meantime his fledgling family business was lost, and all the equipment was repossessed.

While convalescing, Dad had to devise a plan for the financial survival of our family. By that time, I was already earning money for myself by serving meal trays at the hospital, mowing lawns, trimming trees, sacking groceries, and occasionally caddying at the golf course. Dad decided delivering newspapers was a steady, year-round job suitable for Taylor and me that could be passed down to Deb and Donna when they got old enough. All the income from our paper routes went towards family support.

For the rest of his life, Dad was careful not to overexert his fragile heart with physical labor. Consequently, all the heavy or strenuous labor that fathers normally shouldered fell on my mother and me. Ironically, when he had quadruple bypass surgery at the age of 70, all his test results indicated he hadn't actually had a heart attack in 1957. But my father refused to believe the new findings because he was convinced his previous episode had been a life-threatening heart attack, and he had lived his life accordingly.

The Birds and the Bees

My dad never said a word to me about sex. All the guidance I received came from my mom. She used my love for my sisters to teach me to respect girls. She pointed out that every girl was someone's sister and I needed to treat those girls the way I wanted other boys to treat my sisters. Whenever I saw a guy mistreating a girl, I could never look the other way because I loved my mother and my sisters.

I was only in my early teens when my mom told me, "All Gillespie men are good lovers."

I felt as if I had been issued a challenge to uphold the honor of my Gillespie ancestors by carrying on our proud family tradition. But being armed with only a library card, that was a hard reputation to live up to!

Mom's final word on sex came one night when I was in high school.

She followed me to my car as I was about to leave on a date and said, "You'd better behave yourself."

She headed back to the house, changed her mind, turned around, and came back to my car. She bent down so she could see me through the passenger window and looked me straight in the eye. "Do you know what I mean?"

I couldn't believe that she was pushing the issue, and I indignantly answered, "YES!"

"You keep your pants on!"

It was really shocking to have my mother talk so frankly to me about sex.

Goose Is Short for Goose-yah-me

The direction of my entire life changed one night at a parent-teacher conference. The band director shattered my parents' hopes that I had inherited natural musical ability. He told them I had no musical aptitude and suggested I should simply be allowed to play football instead. I was so thrilled to trade band for football. There was never a happier boy!

Football was my game. I was happy to be big and strong and part of a team. A kid on my team nicknamed me 'Goose-yah-me' when he couldn't remember Gillespie. My buddies liked the nickname and eventually shortened it to Goose. At a high school pep rally my senior year, the cheerleaders called my team onto the platform and surprised me by having Miss Willie knight me Sir Goose. Suddenly I was a hero, and all the kids knew my name. Everything was going my way during my junior and senior years, and my confidence went through the roof. Playing varsity ball for Tascosa High School was the sweetest time of my life.

Going From the Top to the Bottom

I dated my high school sweetheart through my senior year of high school and first year of college. When she dropped out of high school and wanted to get married, we did. A few months later, we moved to southern California. We were young and healthy, I was making a good living working nights in a grocery warehouse, and I bought us a 1961, red Thunderbird hardtop convertible. We had a beautiful baby girl, and I thought we had the world by the tail!

After a year of trying to have a second child, my wife changed her mind about being a stay-at-home mom and decided to pursue a career. One night, she said she had to work late so we should get a sitter; I could enjoy a night out with the guys and shoot some pool. It sounded like a great idea. I picked up a buddy from work and we played pool all evening. As the night wore on, we became concerned that my wife might be having car trouble since she still wasn't home from work. This was back before cell phones, so we went to check on her. Her shop was closed, so we drove around until I spotted her car in the parking lot of a bar. As we pulled up, my headlights lit the inside of her car, and I saw her. She was exposed and in the arms of her boss. There are no words to express...

I had absolutely trusted my wife. I believed we would have other children and build a happy home together. I stayed in California for a year hoping we'd be able to work things out. I was miserable being separated from my daughter. Finally, I moved back to Texas, but even that didn't help. We had been married 6 years and my daughter was 4 when we got our divorce. I was at the end of my rope and without any place to go. Our country was deep in the Vietnam War, and I tried to enlist in the service. They refused to accept me because I had dependents. Even the army didn't want me. I had gone from the very top to the very bottom. Never before had I felt so useless and helpless.

If they lock you away, does that make you a Little Princess?

When my dad got out of the service, he found a job as a heavy equipment operator. He worked on the pipeline built across Texas in the early 50s. We moved every few weeks. We lived in a trailer small enough to pull behind our car. My parents carried a role of picket fence to make a small, safe play area for me in each place we lived. Sometimes my mom put a harness on me. People told her she shouldn't put her little girl on a leash like a dog, but Mom insisted it was for my safety.

When I started school, we put down roots in Odessa, Texas. Dad went into business for himself, and things really changed. We got a larger trailer, and Dad staked my picket fence down permanently. We lived in a trailer park where I was seldom allowed out of my yard. If kids came over, they weren't allowed to go into our house for any reason; they couldn't go in to look for toys, because it was hot outside, for a drink of water, or to go to the bathroom. And I wasn't allowed to freely go in and out of my house either. In fact, I had to knock and wait for my mother to answer the door so I could *ask* to go inside to the bathroom or to have a drink of water. I longed for children to come into my yard and play with me. It seldom happened, and when it did it was short lived. Eventually I gave up the idea of friends and concentrated on praying for a brother or sister to play with. I was 9 when my only sister, Johnye, was born. I loved having a live baby doll, but being almost 10 years apart meant we didn't have very much in common. Johnye was only 9 when I married and moved away. It wasn't until both our parents were gone that I realized she was my true inheritance. She was 40 and I was 50 when we became close.

Individuals or a Family

Growing up, I considered myself a daddy's girl. When I was little, he was the one who played with me the most, and when I got older, we could talk about *practically* anything. My dad was a lot of fun, but my mother was no fun! She complained that she had to be the disciplinarian while my dad got to be the good guy. My parents never seemed like a good match to me. They had entirely different attitudes, values, and lives. Dad went to bed early and got up early. Mom watched TV until the station went off the air and slept until almost noon. I was always free to go to bed whenever I wanted. Even in elementary school I set my own alarm clock, got up by myself, and dressed. There was money left on my dresser to buy breakfast, which was always a Coke and a candy bar.

My parents weren't affectionate with one another or with me; there were no farewells or warm welcomes, no getting tucked in bed or listening to prayers, and certainly no hugs and kisses. When I was 8, we took one family vacation to Disneyland. After that, my parents went on separate vacations with friends rather than with one another. The only thing I remember my parents doing together was attending Sunday morning church and going out to eat afterwards.

Strange Behavior

We didn't invite people to our home, and we weren't guests in theirs. In fact, the shock of having a visitor threw my mother into a panic. If we happened to be eating and someone from the church knocked on our door, we flew into action stashing all the food in the oven and plates out of sight in the sink. I'm sure bootleggers had nothing on us when it came to hiding evidence. Eventually, we started eating in the dark on church visitation nights so we wouldn't have to answer the door.

My parents told 2 stories that explained our family's solitary life. A couple came over and allowed their son to destroy the holsters to my cowboy pistol with a pair of scissors while both his parents and my parents watched. My dad cracked under the pressure. Out of his frustration he spanked me without a reason.

My mom exploded and told him, "Kay has done nothing wrong. You're just spanking her because we're all sitting around like a bunch of idiots not saying a word while this brat cut up her holster. She doesn't deserve a spanking, everyone else does!"

The story goes that the parents snatched up their son and never returned.

In the second story, Dad came home from work, and Mom didn't have dinner ready because a lady had been over visiting all afternoon. In front of the woman, Dad told Mother she ought to have his dinner ready and on the table and the other woman ought to be home cooking for her own husband. Again, the guest stomped out our front door in a huff.

Life Went from Bad to Worse to Wonderful!

School was *hard*. I had a reversal problem. I couldn't tell my right from my left, the direction to unscrew a lid, or "b" from "d". One teacher kept me in during recess to do extra work and slapped my leg with a ruler every time I made a mistake. Another teacher walked by my desk, noticed me making a mistake, and hit my knuckles with a stick of chalk so hard that it broke into pieces. Later, she wrote all the misspelled words from one of my papers on the board, and the class laughed at me. My parents refused to get involved and insisted it would be worse for me if they interfered.

I was the biggest kid in my class. The boys made fun of me on the playground, and I spent a lot of time in the principal's office for fighting. I knew the school office called my mom about my fights, but no one told me how she responded, and at home she never mentioned it.

My mom was disappointed when I outgrew being a cute, little blonde. When we shopped, she was always angry, and I didn't understand why. She embarrassed me when she made critical comments about my size in front of the store clerks. I could have used an understanding and sympathetic adult to help me cope, but my mother was neither.

I wasn't athletic. When team captains selected who would be on their side, I was the last one picked. I didn't get picked for the school choir. Mom wouldn't let me take dance lessons. No one invited me to birthday parties or sleepovers. I didn't join clubs, take lessons, or babysit anyone except Johnye. So being isolated in my front yard as a preschooler was lonely, but not nearly as miserable and lonely as going to school and finding rejection.

My sixth grade school year was underway when Melanie joined our class. I still remember how uncomfortable she looked standing there at the front of the room while being introduced. She looked tiny to me. She weighed 72 pounds to my 144. The teacher asked for a volunteer to share their locker with the new girl. Mel thought it was strange that I stretched my hand high and waved it frantically, since I was the only one who even held up a hand. She didn't know how much I needed someone, even if they had to be assigned to me. We became friends, and having just one friend took my life from the bottom to the top.

My parents really liked Mel, and she was always welcome at our house. We even got to spend the night together. I was practically becoming a regular kid. My mom put me on a diet that year at mid-semester, and by the start of junior high school, I had lost 24 pounds. Losing that weight caused a wonderful change in my life and attitude. I couldn't have lost the weight without my mother, and it really helped our relationship to be on the same team. Years later when I was married and had children, Mother and I became the best of friends.

At Tascosa High School I remained an outsider, but it was painless because of Melanie. She and I were the 2 nerdy girls. We shopped together, and since we had similar tastes, it wasn't unusual for us to buy the same outfits and dress alike. We loved it when the teachers started calling us the Bobbsey Twins. The greatest day came when her Presbyterian parents allowed her to join my little Baptist church. We truly were inseparable because I wouldn't go anywhere unless Mel could join me. My happy teen years seemed to erase all the hurtful memories of my childhood. I was stunned when her dad announced that he was moving their family to Palestine, Texas, the week following our graduation. Suddenly my good life was over and there I was, all alone again!

Different Trees but the Same Roots!

Obviously, Ron's happy memories of school and friends weren't the same as mine. He was so happy to be big and strong, but I was self-conscious about my size. It's soothing to listen to Ron reminisce about his childhood; it makes me smile. Though our childhoods were different, our folks had similar parenting styles. Our spit-fire mothers carried big sticks, ruled the roost, and demanded blind obedience. Our fathers were passive and hid in the background. When we discuss our home life and the rules we had growing up, we can easily relate.

I'll always remember my mother telling me, "I love you whether you're good or bad but other people won't love you if you're bad. I want others to love you as much as I do and that's why I make you behave." Her explanation shaped my attitude about people in authority, their rules, and the consequences.

Ron and I are grateful for our families and that we grew up in the innocent era of the 50s. It seems that parents had a great deal of help from schools, media, and the community as they instilled morals and values in young people. We consider our childhoods to be a perpetual blessing.

A Ready-Made Family

The Decision of a Broken Man

After my divorce I eventually landed in Houston, Texas, where I worked nights in a grocery warehouse. After my shift, I usually went with my work buddies to the bar to have a couple of beers and shoot pool. One morning after my friends went home, I was sitting at the bar by myself when the day barmaid came to work. I could see her putting on makeup and fixing her hair. I asked if she always waited until she came to work before she got dressed. And before the conversation was finished, I had asked this total stranger for a date. I was 28, and she was 33.

Little did I know that in some respects, this woman would remain a stranger after 39 years because I would know next-to-nothing about her past. It's hard to believe I never met a single member of her family. I only met one person from her past, and that was her youngest son's father. But when I asked him, he couldn't tell me any more than the little I already knew. He had never met any of Betty's family or even one of her friends.

When I moved to Houston and met Betty, I was a broken man. I didn't choose Betty. I didn't court her. I made no attempt to win her heart. And I *never* proposed to her. After Betty ran away from home at 15, failed at 2 marriages, and had 3 sons, she was just as untrusting as I was.

That was how we started out.

What Dads Do 😊

Betty's boys were living with her ex-mother-in-law. One day, about the time school let out, there was a knock at the front door and, to my surprise, it was her 2 oldest sons: Jim, age 12, and Joe, age 10. Her preschool son, Rick, still lived with his dad and was not with the older 2. Before that day, all 3 boys had been to my apartment only once to swim.

When we asked them how they got to my apartment, their only answer was, "We found it."

The boys started asking questions. One thing led to another, and before I knew it, they were asking Betty, "What do we call him?"

We told them they could call me anything they liked. And they decided to call me Dad.

I was tired of the life I'd been leading since I returned to Texas as a single man. I wanted to do something worthwhile, and Betty's 3 sons needed some male guidance – so there was my answer. I was convinced that my leadership experience with younger boys in scouts and being Taylor's older brother had prepared me to be a positive influence and make a difference in the lives of Jim, Joe, and Rick. It wasn't too long before we moved to Denver, Colorado, and I put her boys in a scout troop and became their scout master. The values I'd learned in boy scouts were powerful guides in my life, and I was confident her boys could benefit from scouting as well. But they hated the scouts. Much to my embarrassment, they were uncooperative and whenever there was a problem, it was caused by my boys.

I finally allowed Jim and Joe to drop out of scouts, but I wasn't through. I'd thrown newspapers for years. So naturally, that was a job I thought I could teach them. In the 6 years I threw papers, there were times I had as many as 3 routes to throw before school. I thought a paper route could help them develop a work ethic, earn their own money, and learn to manage it. Again, I was wrong. It was a total disaster. Before the first month was up, I found myself repaying the newspaper out of my paycheck that could barely support my new family of 5.

Only Pretending 😊

In the beginning with Betty, one small step and one convenient white lie led to another. We presented ourselves as a married couple and before long found ourselves in an unexpected place. Rick's father was the only one who ever questioned us. When he did, Betty altered their marriage license to look as if it was ours and convincingly waved it in his face while they were arguing.

When the time came to move back to Amarillo and live around my family, we thought it would be easiest to continue to present ourselves as a married couple. Betty asked me to buy her a wedding ring for appearances, and she decided to use her birthdate as our wedding date so she could keep her story straight.

17 Years on an Iffy Road 😊

On our first date, Betty drank until she passed out. I had firmly made up my mind when I was a young boy, because of Uncle Warren's example, that I never wanted alcohol to take over and ruin my life. So, I immediately lost interest in Betty. The next day she called me, apologized, and insisted she didn't have a drinking problem. After she moved in and her boys arrived, I told Betty that we needed to provide a sober and stable place where the boys could grow up. I found it was an impossible standard to maintain, and her drinking continued to have ups and downs.

Years later, Betty told people that she used to be an alcoholic, but Jesus took away her desire to drink. That was true for a time, but it didn't last. Drinking became a cycle. We'd go a little while without alcohol in our home, and then it would gradually creep back in. When it became a threat I'd put my foot down, and she would stop drinking again. One of her longest dry spells was brought to an end when my sister and her husband told Betty they had a glass of wine every evening and it was healthy. Betty clung to that argument, and I could never again convince her that her drinking was a problem. Over the course of our marriage, Betty's medications grew steadily and the combination of alcohol with her medications increased their influence. There were times she'd have as much as 2 16-ounce tumblers of wine. She'd be slurring her speech and wobbling, but even then she insisted that she hadn't drunk enough to be effected at all. I was always grateful that at least Betty was careful with her drinking when we were out in public or around my family.

Between Betty's drinking and her 2 oldest sons rejecting all my efforts to guide their lives, it was a rocky relationship. I found my-self taking on the heavy burden of Betty's medical expenses that continually grew over the years. We were plagued by collection calls. To keep the wolf from the door, we were making small monthly payments to hospitals and numerous doctors. Take all of that and add it to dealing with her mistrust and suspicions due to her 2 previous husbands, and there you have my life.

I Had a Dream

To tell the truth, the first 4 or 5 years we were together I was holding out a grain of hope in the back of my mind that someday my ex-wife would return with our daughter, ask for my forgiveness, and we could build the good life I'd imagined since I was a kid in high school. Eventually, I accepted my life the way it was. Still, I *never* gave up wishing I could raise my own daughter.

Betty and I were not married, but we allowed everyone to believe that we were. When we did feel guilty, we would justify it as a common law marriage. After 17 years of living together, I won a trip to Las Vegas. That provided the perfect opportunity for us to secretly marry at a small wedding chapel, and we finally came out from under the guilt.

Who was that stranger? 😊

In the 39 years Betty and I were together, she never had a phone call, a birthday present, or a Christmas card from her family. I had no family names or numbers to contact the day she died. Over the years, Betty was questioned casually as well as intentionally by me, her 3 sons, and members of my family, but she refused to answer our questions. Even the few insignificant things that slipped out over the years seemed more like wishful thinking than facts. None of it fit together or made any sense.

Recalling my life with Betty for this book has been difficult. During our marriage, my life as a family man was too demanding for me to stop, step back, and take a good look at what we had and the direction we were headed. During all those hectic years, learning about Betty's past wasn't a burning desire I woke up with every morning. I lived with her innocently thinking our marriage was good, close, and would grow even closer. But I see now that she deliberately allowed me to believe whatever I wanted, even when she knew it was a lie.

As we became more committed Christians, the secretive part

of Betty's life was never affected. One particular sermon on forgiveness moved me. I assumed Betty would feel the same way. I suggested that she forgive her family and reconcile their relationships. When I mentioned contacting her family, she instantly became furious and told me, if that was what church was all about, then she was ready to quit going. We could just stay home and forget everything. I was shocked!

She often told me, "The only family I want or need is your family. Your mother is my mother, and your sisters are my sisters."

She always maintained that her relationship with me was plenty. I wish I had asked her, "Betty, when you keep your life a secret from me, exactly what kind of life do you think that we have?"

Betty Jane and My Dad

When Betty came into our family, she was not well received by my dad. I'm quite sure that he saw Betty and her 3 sons as an albatross around my neck. At family gatherings, Dad was openly affectionate toward his 4 daughters and his other daughter-in-law, Sandie, but Betty might as well have been invisible.

When Dad's health started failing and he was in the first stages of Alzheimer's, the doctor took his driver's license away. Eventually, Mom and Dad felt like prisoners in their own home. One evening, my mom asked if Dad could spend the next day at his old office so she could get away for a while. I agreed to keep an eye on him for her. It worked. Dad was no trouble, and Mom had a little freedom. Initially our entire family pulled together to transport Dad to and from the office every day. But over time, it became harder and harder to coordinate everyone's schedules.

One day, Betty told my mom she would pick Dad up, let him ride with her to the post office and bank, and then he could stay at the office until she finished her work. Then she'd bring him back home. From that day on, Dad became a 5-day-a-week chore for Betty. She'd take Dad to his old office, seat him behind his desk, fetch him a cup of coffee, and he'd sit there as happy as could be. He never interfered with business. He'd gaze at the things on the wall or open his drawer and look at whatever was in there. I believe he was happy just to be on the premises and be aware of the office activity.

Soon Dad's attitude completely changed and he thought Betty hung the moon. He was big on nicknames, and he changed Betty Ann to Betty Jane. Clearly, Dad finally accepted Betty.

He said repeatedly, "That Betty Jane is quite a gal."

I asked Betty, "Isn't it great that Dad likes you so much?"

Her response was, "Yes, after all these years he acts as if he likes me, but it would have meant so much more if he could have done it when he had his full mind."

Looking back, in the beginning Betty drove Dad to the office more for my mom than for my dad. She wouldn't accept any money for gas, and she never took a day off from her newfound responsibility. My dad had it right, that Betty Jane was quite a gal.

I Got What I Asked For

I Was an Old Maid

After we graduated and Mel moved, I didn't know what to do with myself. That summer, I got better at going places without my running buddy, but I didn't like it. I wished Mel had been around, and maybe we could have gotten jobs together. All I wanted to do was move out of my parent's house, marry, and start my adult life as a wife and mother, but there wasn't a husband candidate in sight. There were no boys at my church, I hadn't enrolled in college, I had no friends, and I had only been to one party in my life; so, I was clearly going to be an old maid. Hopeless at 18, I talked to my local recruiter. I thought, *Surely the army would take good care of me, or at least they wouldn't let me starve, go naked, or sleep in a dumpster.* I fully intended to enlist.

In the meantime, my dad's friend, Roy, offered to introduce me to his 3 cowboy nephews. He said I could have a look and take my pick. I met them all that week and selected cowboy number 2, Johnny Crownover, to be my husband.

It Was Fast

After 9 weeks, we had decided to marry but we had no reason to be in a hurry or even set a date. Everything changed when I got fired from my job. I knew I wouldn't be able to make my car payment, and I was afraid to tell my parents. When John came over that Friday night, I asked him if we could hurry up and get married so I wouldn't have to look for another job in Amarillo.

He just shrugged his shoulders and said, "Okay."

Since John was that easy to convince, I knew I'd found my man! Without any further plans or discussion, we told my parents we were getting married in 5 days. They didn't handle it well, but we stuck by our guns. The wedding plans came together in an hour. I asked Mel and Sonja to wear yellow dresses if they owned one. John and his groomsmen were mismatched as well, wearing their old suits or sports jackets. Since we didn't have a rehearsal dinner, his parents bought our wedding cake. We had 2 little floral arrangements, one for the piano and one for the organ that we also used on the reception table. I let the organist select my music.

Our invitation was a single Sunday morning announcement, "If you'd like to see Kay Sharp marry Johnny Crownover, come an hour early for the Wednesday night Thanksgiving Dinner."

That was it. Short, sweet, and to the point!

My mom wasn't happy with my barebones wedding, but she had missed her chance if she wanted something more. I'd tried to get her to look at bride magazines with me earlier, but she blew me off. I thought, *My life had been at a dead end since graduation; this was my big opportunity, and I wasn't going to postpone it just so she could add fluff.*

The night before the wedding, she asked John if it bothered him that I'd bought a short white dress for the wedding.

In true Johnny Crownover style, he innocently answered, "I thought all brides had to wear long white dresses, but if she wants a short one that's fine with me."

I quietly slipped away by myself a few hours before the wedding and bought a long, white dress. When my dad walked me down the aisle, John and my mother were both pleasantly surprised. When we reached the place where my dad was supposed to stop and give my hand to John, I froze in mid-stride. I never got enough courage to pull my back foot forward and place it beside my front foot. I stood there wobbling and never heard a single word the preacher said. I was realizing a little too late that *I really didn't know this boy. All I needed was someone to make my car payment, but here I was getting married instead.*

When the preacher asked me, "Do you take this man to be your lawfully wedded husband?" I couldn't speak!

Instead, I closed my eyes and just moaned. Everything was a blur. I was having my last-minute jitters during the wedding. In my wedding photos, I'm staring expressionless into space. All I could think was, *What have I done? And what will I be expected to do in just a little while with this TOTAL STRANGER?*

Milk and Jam

My dad's sex talks came in the form of 2 *Dear Abby* articles left with a $20 bill on the corner of my dresser. I still remember both of them.

"You don't buy a cow if you can milk her through the fence," and "The peach that's the easiest to pick gets in the jam first."

V Stands for...

Until my wedding day, my mom's sex talks had been, "You know what's right, *so do it!*" and that had kept me a virgin.

I suppose she thought I might need a little something extra for my honeymoon.

The day of the wedding, I was rushing around with last-minute deliveries and details, nervous and sick to my stomach! I packed in my spare time between running errands and making certain I hadn't forgotten anything. My little 9-year-old sister kept messing with my stuff. Finally, I told my mom that I was going to thump her if she didn't stay out of my cosmetic bag. Mother asked what she was doing, and I said she kept putting a giant jar of Vaseline in my suitcase.

Mother said, "Johnye didn't put it in there, I did."

I asked her, "What for?"

She said, "Just in case you need it."

"Mom, how can I need it if I don't know what it's for?"

My mother had spent all my life avoiding this conversation, and she wasn't going to relent this close to the finish line.

"Take it just in case John needs it."

"What for?" I persisted.

"You never know," was her lengthy explanation.

"Well, if he needs it he can just bring it himself!"

At this point, my mother covered her face and was practically in tears, "Kay, I haven't asked you for much. Can't you do this one thing for me?"

Since she was cracking up, I decided to drop the subject, give in, and take the stupid jar of Vaseline. In the motel, when we started unpacking, I pulled the great big thing out of my suitcase and said to John, "Oh yeah, my mom sent this jar of Vaseline for you."

To which my worldly-wise young husband replied, "What for?"

"Mom said you might need it."

"Really, for what?"

"I don't know. She wouldn't say but she seemed to think you'd know what it was for."

On my honor, Johnny Crownover said, "Well, at our house we use it for chapped lips," and we both took a tiny smidgen and dabbed it on our lips. But we didn't need it.

It took a while before there were fireworks, but in the meantime, we proved to ourselves and to one another what we were made of. Despite being virtual teenage strangers, we did pretty darn good.

He was the right man for the hour. He was understanding, unselfish, and patient to a fault. I loved and respected him for putting my feelings before his own, and I always will.

My Heartless Love for Jesus

I invited Jesus to come into my heart when I was 7. Unlike many adults who doubt their childhood salvation experience, I never have. I did not go forward after a hellfire and brimstone sermon, with my little friends, or because an adult was pressuring me. One Sunday, the sermon was on giving and the preacher asked all the people who tithed to join hands and form a circle around the sanctuary as a show of their faith and commitment. When the service was over, I was crying because I realized that I wasn't a tither. My parents tried to comfort me by telling me that I was a tither if they were. I didn't accept their answer. From that I also figured out I wasn't a believer just because my parents were believers, so I went forward on my own. I prayed and asked Jesus to come into my life and never leave me. He never has.

I had a horrible experience during my teen years that stopped me from growing as a Christian. I didn't dance, play cards, smoke, drink, or "fool around". Because I avoided that list of sins, I was absolutely convinced that I was a model Christian. When John and I got married he'd been out of church for years, and I hauled his little butt right back to the pew. I had him tithing, carrying his Bible, and going to Sunday school before he knew what happened. I was an awesome Christian wife!

Back then, there were bookmarks and bumper stickers that

said, "If you were the only sinner in the world, Jesus would die just for you!" I used to think, *Heck, if I were the only sinner then Jesus wouldn't need to die. He could just have a slight headache for a few minutes.* I felt heaven was fortunate to have someone of my caliber on their team. I was a full-blown Pharisee. I saw myself as practically sinless, and everyone else as far beneath me.

One night during a revival service, I saw people weeping and going to the altar for prayer. I remember standing there as cold as a rock and thinking to myself, *I wish I felt something instead of boredom. I almost envy them.* I didn't consider that a prayer but obviously God did because suddenly it happened. I saw the truth about myself. I was stunned as I realized that I wasn't sinless. I was arrogant, self-righteous, ungrateful, and unloving. Jesus *had* needed to die for my sins!

At 7 I knew I was a sinner, but so was everyone else. The Bible said everyone was a sinner, but I couldn't come up with any specific sin I had committed. I considered being a sinner was like being white, I was born that way. But that night, I got the message I was a sinner because of my sin. Forget that I didn't play cards or smoke, I was a pious hypocrite who felt deserving of a privileged life. I realized the religious people who crucified Jesus were the same as I was. With genuine shame for my snobbish attitude, I went to the altar. It was a beautiful experience though I didn't understand why. That was the first time I felt His great love without feeling that I deserved it.

Later, I read that Jesus said, "He who is forgiven little, loves little," and then I understood my transformation.

It was true. I didn't have much love for a savior who had a slight headache for a couple of minutes to pay for my few small sins, but I had love beyond measure for the savior who suffered and died because of my pious heart. The debt I owed but could not pay, Jesus paid on my behalf. That enlarged my capacity to love Him. Knowing He loved me while I was a snob instead of waiting until I changed, proved how great his love was. Finally I understood, and I was the happiest I had ever been.

It had been more than 22 years since I'd prayed and asked Jesus to be the Lord of my life. During those years, I'd attended church faithfully, memorized scripture, and taught Sunday school, but my growth began in earnest the night I saw my sin.

Hennie Penny

When John and I were first married, I only brought snacks and rode the tractor with him. Soon, I started plowing a little and helping with irrigation. Then I got my Commercial Driver's License and drove grain trucks during harvest. For 15 years I had a garden and fruit trees. From the time my children were little, they helped too. They would pick, snap, and shell. I could not have made it without them.

When John sat down in his recliner to watch the game, I brought him a nice, big glass of iced tea, an empty bowl, and a grocery sack full of beans to snap. We were busy! I kept a long to do list. John didn't like helping me and was always in a big hurry to get his boots on and get out of the house. At the farm he was his own boss, he could sit behind a steering wheel and smoke all he wanted. He got up early, dressed, left the house, and never looked back or came home until it was dark. I thought when he was home, he should be helping. I only had thoughts of multitasking but never of relaxing. The very idea of *relaxing* was ridiculous. *Relaxing* was only for pathetic, lazy people. It was one thing to fall exhausted and muddy into the tub before going to bed, but to sit with legs crossed and arms folded while so much needed to be done was unthinkable! At my house, no one got to ride the clock, and I'm certain that I kept my family worn out, miserable, and on the look-out for a place to hide.

After 10 years of marriage, I got the bug to become a photographer. I went to Amarillo College and did wedding and location photography for 10 years. After that, I started a remodeling business with my friend, Rochelle, which lasted about another 10 years.

I was 50 and the kids were gone when John and I decided to build our dream house. I'd worked on enough houses to know exactly what I wanted. I consulted with the architect and made all the decisions whether great or small. I chose the lot, bricks, rocks, trees, cabinets, stain, baseboards, light fixtures, hardware, Formica, windows, doors, paint colors, wallpaper, carpet, tile, bathroom mirrors, potties, and sinks. I told the electrician where to put the plugs and switches, the plumber where to put faucets, the carpenter how I wanted all the cabinets to look, and I designed our 7 driveways, walkways, and sidewalks. I stood on scaffolding to hand texture, paint, and glaze. I talked and fought with the crew managers when talking and fighting was necessary.

John was rather smug that the only decision he involved himself in was the size of the stairs going to basement. I cared 99.99% about our new house and John cared .01%. But I didn't mind because I was passionate about all those details, and **I wanted the control**. John farmed to pay for the house while he stayed as far away from the job site as possible. He knew that he liked every house we had ever owned, and he would like our new one if I was satisfied with it. So, he farmed, and I built the house.

Typical

After 30 years of marriage, the kids were grown and married, the vegetable garden was no more, we had a housekeeper, and John stopped smoking, but we were still in the habit of being apart all day every day. Nothing changed. I didn't know where he went or what he did while he was away from the house, and when he came home, he seldom asked me what I'd been up to or who I'd talked to. That was our relationship, and we were both okay with it.

Sometimes I got a little goodbye peck and "love you" as we parted. The only time we sat side by side was on the pew at church. When we walked together we didn't hold hands. John loved to 2-step, but my church was against dancing; I never learned how to dance, and he didn't teach me. We only slow danced in our living room one time, and I thought it was very romantic and the perfect beginning to our intimate night. But neither of us ever pursued a second dance.

I was satisfied with John. We agreed on most things. We were faithful and respectful to one another. We were so busy with the farm and the kids that we fell in bed exhausted at night. Intimacy was made from leftover energy at night in the few moments before we fell asleep. I saw it as my gift to him. I knew if anything was going to change in that department, it would have to be me who searched for an answer and did the changing. John wasn't the type to listen or to go along with change even if he was dissatisfied. His attitude was, "If you're unhappy, then you fix it because I'm okay."

I wished we'd sit beside one another at the house instead of in separate recliners, and he would put his arm around my shoulder. I wished sometimes when we walked we could hold hands, and on Valentine's Day or our anniversary, I'd love for him to really kiss me. One evening, could we try to dance again? I'd like to learn how just enough so we could dance at home. If I had said all of this, John would have thought I was trying to pick a fight. The screenwriter for the movie *Hope Springs* could have been a fly on our wall.

The "Other Man" 🙂

When I went back to college to become a wedding photographer, the most experienced student photographer in my class was Mike. He was far more helpful with our lab work than the instructor. Several of us would go on break together, and I went from respecting and admiring Mike's photography to being smitten. I tried not to show how flattered I was when he mentioned that he always noticed how I dressed. When he looked over my shoulder at my prints in the darkroom, he stood closer than was necessary, and he breathed on my neck. Once he leaned in tight, took a long, deep breath and whispered in my ear how good my hair smelled. Oh dear God, how much I longed to be admired, and it didn't matter if it was a compliment on my photography or the smell of my hair. I'd long ago accepted that sweet words had vanished from my life **forever**. I was a 30-year-old mother of 3 who'd been married 10 years. I was a "has been". But Mike let me know that wasn't the way he saw me. I craved attention and compliments. More than anything, I wanted to feel good and confident about something in my life.

This was when I had the biggest struggle of my life where my thoughts were concerned. I will be forever grateful that I was never alone with Mike. Our conversations seldom strayed far from photography, and when it did, it was about his hitch in the service or about my children. We were completely appropriate. But I found myself wondering what Mike might say this week about my photographs or my outfit or the smell of my new shampoo. I took a fantasy vacation from my household duties to dream about a man who said nice things to me.

I've never surprised myself more than when I called Mel and Kathy and asked them to pray for me because I was being tempted.

God has never surprised me more either. The very next time I went to class, Mike tried to borrow a pencil from me during the lecture. He was being his usual flirty self. But this time, for the first time, I saw his behavior as a bother and a nuisance. I went from having a big crush on Mike to being 100% over him. The hold was broken, and the fog had lifted.

While I was toying with my thoughts of Mike, I told myself nothing was going to happen, and even if it did, no one would ever know. Probably the only person who might ever find out would be John. And I would tell him, "You didn't wait until you married like I did. So you owe me one." I actually thought that would justify everything. What else could John do but be *a good sport* about it? It wasn't until the spell was broken that I realized if anything had happened, sooner or later everyone would have heard about it; my children, my parents, my friends, and my church. The true magnitude of the consequences had never occurred to me, but when reality finally set in, I understood that the costs would have been staggering. I must have been out of my mind to even entertain those thoughts.

I'm always amazed that I was so casual and so deceived. I toyed with the annihilation of my character for a compliment. I looked the same, and my hair smelled the same whether anyone noticed or complimented me. But I felt so good when someone did!

I knew, *even though I'd done nothing wrong, I would always feel guilty for my thoughts.* When my children got old enough for me to talk to them about purity, I wouldn't be able to because I'd feel like a hypocrite. What could I do that would set me free? I couldn't take back my daydreams. I had all kinds of thoughts and emotions going on inside me. I wanted to talk to someone and try to sort through them. The last person in the world I wanted to confide in was John, but he had a right to know. It wasn't any of my friends' business. It was John's business. The 2 of us had everything to lose. We needed to be a team against anything that threatened our home. I wanted to honestly spread out all the pieces and for the 2 of us to look at them together. After all, we wanted to take every precaution against this type of temptation ever coming up again, didn't we? As a Christian wife, I thought telling John was the honorable way to handle it.

So that same night, after I put the kids to bed, I sat down on the couch with John and told him about the temptation I'd been under. I told John that Mike and I went on break with the other students, and everyone mainly talked about photography, but I was having a problem because I looked so forward to the nice things Mike said to me practically every day.

It wasn't Mike but the compliments that seduced me. I wanted to feel loved and admired again instead of feeling old and washed-up. If my husband didn't say sweet things to me, then I was an easy target for temptation. I didn't tell John to hurt him, blame him, or threaten him. I just thought if he knew what I was up against, he would want to help me. After all, the solution was as simple as saying, "I love you. You sure look nice today, honey. I'm so glad you're mine." Surely my sweet husband would want to rescue me.

I asked John to forgive me. I asked him to please start saying the things I needed to hear so it would help me in the future. I was a little nervous. I wasn't sure what to expect. John never spoke. He didn't storm off. He didn't reach over and take my hand. He didn't say, "I'm glad you told me," or "I wish you hadn't told me." He didn't say, "I'm glad you didn't do it." "If this ever happens again we are through." "You and the kids are my life." "You're never going back to class." "I understand because I've been tempted too."

John never said a single word, and in the 26 years following my confession, he never once brought it up.

He didn't start saying sweet things either. Once, he did call and leave a message on the answering machine. He said I looked nice that day when I brought meals to the field. I never erased that message, and I played it often…in the beginning. After a while, the electricity went off in a lighting storm, and the message got erased.

Looking back, it's easy to see how we were both too busy. We didn't share passions, and even when I spoke plain and explained how close our marriage had come to a disaster, he still didn't speak. What he communicated to me was, "It's your problem. *You fix it.*" The only way I knew to survive was to convince myself that John was the normal one. My need for compliments and words of affirmation and love was just plain silly. I needed to grow up and get over it.

I stayed faithful to my marriage because I loved God and I loved John. I wanted my children to grow up in a home with both their biological parents. I wanted to keep my integrity for the sake of my own sanity.

I knew then and I know now that John loved me. I believe he was the right man for me to marry, and I'm glad that I did. I knew our marriage was better than most. I always knew our marriage could have been better, but it wasn't going to change.

We lost sight of enjoying one another's company. Over the years, we inched apart until we could barely see one another over the mountain of good, great, and wonderful things that soaked up our time. Neither of us objected. I went off with the kids or my friends from church, and he went off to the farm or with the guys from the Co-op. Bottom line – we both went off, and we never got around to coming back. We lived an unspoken agreement where he provided the living, and I provided the rest. We were satisfied to be busy and married to someone who was dependable to do their part. We were typical.

Neither of us was broken-hearted. We weren't worried about our marriage. There was no blame. Neither of us seemed to care that we were drifting apart, and we didn't want a divorce because we were just another normal couple who outgrew the honeymoon stage. We got into a rhythm and became numb to what was happening to our marriage.

And that was fine…*until a person like Mike showed up to remind me of what I was missing.*

So This Is a Dream Vacation

Betty and I went on our dream vacation between Christmas and New Year's to the Grand Old Opry Hotel in Nashville. I didn't know it, but Betty had been greatly impressed by Max, an older gentleman she occasionally visited with who liked to play the part of the rich and famous. He bragged to her about making hotels and restaurants live up to his expectations because, "After all, you're paying for it." Betty bought his story, and she could hardly wait to crack her whip and do the same. This was the most expensive hotel stay of my entire life at $350 per night. As soon as we got in our room, Betty started thoroughly inspecting everything. Our accommodations were far beyond anything I'd ever experienced. Our balcony overlooked a breathtaking scene of fountains, gardens, and bridges. I couldn't believe it.

But something even more unbelievable was on the horizon just as Max had coached her; Betty deemed the room as unacceptable because of the little things she managed to find. She told me that I needed to call the front desk and demand a new room right away. I couldn't believe her. I was good with the room. Furthermore, a new room would probably be just the same as this one. If she was so on fire, she could call them herself. She called them and explained that our room was unacceptable, and she wasn't going to pay this price for a room with these flaws. The front desk was very gracious and apologetic. Within an hour, we were packing up our stuff, and the bellboy was helping us move. I'm sure Betty felt just like Scarlet O'Hara. The next room was identical, and she quickly scanned it and found nothing wrong. She was satisfied that they had bowed to her snobbish demands, and she got to play the part of someone powerful. She also knew me, and the next stunt would mean her dream vacation would be over and we'd be packing up and going home.

As soon as we went downstairs, Betty started complaining that she couldn't walk through such a massive hotel with the shops and restaurants if she had to carry her portable oxygen. When I carried it, we were awkwardly linked together with 5 feet of tubing. I saw an advertisement for "medical mobility rentals," so I rented Betty a scooter, and she was overjoyed that she'd no longer have to walk and lug an oxygen bottle. I cautioned her about the speed. I explained about the tortoise and hare symbols on the handle and told her not to take it off slow because there were 1,800 guests and the hallways were narrow in places. She promised to drive slowly. She said she was glad to have the scooter, and she was confident she'd never need to go faster than the tortoise.

Thanks to having wheels, she was excited to go over 2 blocks and shop at the massive Opry Land Mall. I asked her how we were going to get there, and she said she could ride her scooter. After a couple of hours, the scooter slowed to a halt. It was out of power, and it would require hours to recharge it. The hotel told me the location of their pickup point and that a shuttle would be there *eventually*. The pickup point was more than 2 blocks away, and I had to bend over and push that heavy, dead scooter the entire way with Betty riding. We waited over an hour for their one shuttle equipped with a lift. When the shuttle finally arrived, I had to help the driver load the dead scooter. Our shopping was over. That was the end of dream vacation day one.

Betty was a stickler for fine dining, and it was typical for her to research and make reservations at the nicest place she could find. She'd made reservations at an Italian restaurant in the hotel just before we needed to leave for the Grand Old Opry Show.

In the meantime, Betty had built up her confidence on her scooter, and she was being sneaky as she increased it to full speed. She was zipping up and down the corridors. I cautioned her several times that she was going to run over somebody and hurt them, but she told me not to worry about it.

At the restaurant, I told the maître d that we had to catch the shuttle bus for the show in one hour. He said he didn't think it would be possible to be seated, order, and eat if we wanted to enjoy our meal and still be able to walk to catch our shuttle in just one hour. I agreed with the maître d that we ought to grab a faster meal, so he and I cancelled our reservations.

Betty and I headed toward the main lobby where the faster, sit-down restaurants were. We had to cross an indoor bridge over scenic fountains and plants. Betty was fuming that the maître d and I went over her head and cancelled her well-made plans. I was walking briskly ahead of her over the bridge because our time was running out. All of a sudden, she ran her scooter up on my heel, and I lost my balance. I stumbled forward and fell, hitting my ribs against the steel handrails. I bounced off and fell backwards onto the floor in excruciating pain. I was knocked unconscious for a short while. When I came to, there was a hotel employee bending over me, and a crowd gathered around us. I could hear Betty screaming at the top of her lungs in the background, "I've killed my husband, I've killed my husband!"

Coming back to consciousness and hearing her scream I thought, *How ridiculous.* I heard a man calmly saying to Betty, "Ma'am, Ma'am, calm down. I don't believe your husband is dead."

I refused to let the hotel paramedics take me in an ambulance to the emergency room. I'd watched the Grand Old Opry my entire life on TV, and I'd seen more emergency rooms than most ambulance drivers. I was going to spend tonight at the show, not in an emergency waiting room.

In great pain I managed to rise from the floor, and I walked gingerly to the shuttle pickup location where we sat in silence while we waited for the bus. Then we rode in silence. Then we took our seats in silence. I watched the show in silence while I tightly held my 3 cracked ribs, trying to barely breathe because of the pain that accompanied just a normal breath of air. But Betty laughed her head off and enjoyed the jokes and singing. She even turned to me every now and then and asked, "What's the matter? Don't you think that's funny?" I won't share what I was really thinking.

The night wasn't a total loss. At intermission I did get to eat my dinner: a box of Jujyfruits and Coke in a small Styrofoam cup.

Sister Do Gooder

In 1972, I moved us to Amarillo to go into business with my dad. Betty made friends with the girl down the street, Karen, a girl I'd gone to school with from the age of 13. Betty started attending Karen's small Baptist church, and they would ask me to go with them. I always told them I had more important things to do, like watch the Dallas Cowboy's pregame show.

Sister Do Gooder, as I referred to Karen, said, "That's okay, boy. We'll just pray you into church."

I told her, "Go ahead. It will be a cold day in Hell when I show up! So have at it. Knock yourself out and pray all you want."

A few months later, I had a near-fatal accident on the road. I was telling Dale, Karen's husband, all about it. He let me finish telling my story, and then he asked me, "Who was with you, Ron?"

I told him, "Nobody."

He asked me again, "Who was with you, Ron?"

"I told you, nobody. I was by myself."

This time he said, "Think about it. Someone was with you."

It finally dawned on me that if God hadn't been with me, I wouldn't have been standing there. The next Sunday, Betty and Sister Do Gooder went off to church together. I showed up later on my own. I'm not sure who was more shocked, them or me. Those 2 girls just looked at one another with great, big smiles on their faces. But they never rubbed it in. I guess they didn't want to undo what God had done.

I Met Jesus in a Little Spearman Motel

There were only about 15 young families attending that little Memorial Baptist Church. Every Sunday morning, they would close the service with endless verses of "Just as I Am", waiting for the lost to come forward. It was no secret; everyone there had walked the aisle, accepted Jesus as their savior, and joined the church except me. I viewed aisle walking and getting saved as some sort of Baptist doctrine. Besides, I knew I didn't need it because my mom had shuffled our entire family down front to join the Methodist church when I was 11-years-old. I was a good person and a Methodist church member. As far as I knew, I was good to go where God was concerned. But more than that, I didn't want to go forward and give them the satisfaction of knowing they wore me down until I finally gave in and did it their way. I just wanted to tell them, "Come on, you know everybody in here's been down front 2 or 3 times already. You're just waiting for me, and I'M NOT COMING! Now, let's all go home and watch the Cowboys play."

A few months later, I was on my sales route and spent the night in a little motel in Spearman, Texas. I was bored, and there was nothing on TV. I looked over on the dresser and there was a Gideon Bible, so I opened it up. There were scriptures to read on various subjects, and salvation was one of them. I looked them up and as I read them, I realized it was in God's word that a person must be unashamed to tell others that they have embraced Jesus. Making a public statement was not just some type of doctrine the Baptists cooked up. Though my mom wanted all her little children in heaven with her someday, she couldn't do it for us and it wasn't being a member of a church that would have gotten us to heaven anyway.

At that point, I felt the presence of God come over me. This was a private thing. Inviting Jesus to be my Lord and Savior didn't have to be in front of a crowd. It was a matter of inviting Jesus to come in and change my heart. I took the words of the scripture literally.

I went back to the little Baptist church the following Sunday and told them I was one of them. I was no longer ashamed, and it wasn't an issue. I told the congregation that I'd given my life to Jesus. Now, hopefully they'd knock off the 10 stanzas of "Just as I Am" and we could all go home and watch the Cowboys in peace.

Betty and I started taking her 3 sons to Sunday school and church, but like the scouts and the newspaper route, the boys didn't want any part of that either. As a young stepfather, my good intentions were frequently met with undesirable results.

Rocking along for 30 Years

My spiritual journey might best be described as a smorgasbord. I was sprinkled as a little boy when my family went forward to join the Methodist church. Years later, I accepted Jesus as my Savior in a motel. The following week, I walked the aisle in a small Baptist Church and made a public profession of my newfound faith. At the time, I was willing to follow the Baptist way of baptizing by immersion, but the little church didn't have a baptistery. I located a baptistery we could have for free, but before we could get it installed, the little church disbanded.

I rocked along for more than 30 years unbaptized by immersion. Jay, my friend and pastor, dogged me about being baptized every chance he got. It wasn't so much that I didn't want to be immersed, as much as I didn't want to give in to his harassment. After I married k, she asked me why I'd never been baptized. I explained that I didn't want to give in to Jay's pressure.

She said, "Are you willing to be disobedient to scripture for no better reason than to stubbornly resist Jay's pressure?" When it was put that way, what could I say? So Jay met us at the church one weekday evening, and k was the one to dunk me. When I was baptized the second time I was an adult, and the decision was all mine. I understood all that it meant, and it meant a lot. This was my obedience to God's command. I didn't do it to get Jay off my back or to pacify k. When I thought about baptism as yielding to the one who died in my place, there was nothing I wouldn't gladly do for him.

A Big Thanks to Dr. Dove & Dr. Sahad

After Betty and I had been together 6 months, we moved to Denver. She told me about the car wreck she was in before we met.

The steering wheel crushed her abdomen, and her injuries had been extensive. She had multiple surgeries and a 3-month hospital stay. Before the end of our first 6 months, her health issues had resurfaced.

Betty was a chain smoker and her lungs collapsed 3 times in a single year. The third time, she had to have her first, major lung surgery. From that point on for the rest of our married life, she had multiple surgeries. She had several abdomen hernia repairs, 2 TMJ (temporomandibular joint) surgeries, a hysterectomy, and a gallbladder surgery to name only a few. Her surgical history was incredible. Our friends and family couldn't believe one person could need so many medical procedures. I'll always wonder if all her surgeries and procedures were actually *necessary*. There are untold years of my life spent in doctors' waiting rooms, surgical waiting rooms, and emergency rooms waiting for the results of tests and x-rays. Most of the time the tests were inconclusive, and we were sent home and told to return the next day for more tests. Eventually, not really knowing what to do for her, they would opt to try a medication, treatment, or procedure. I kept an updated list of her medications on my computer so I could readily print it any time we were referred to a different doctor. Our bills for doctors, tests, medications, and the hospital were never ending. There wasn't any relief in sight until Medicare. And even Medicare didn't fix it for us, but for the first time we were finally seeing a little daylight. Best of all, the bill collection calls stopped. Several things happened about the same time, and they all helped our finances; Betty qualified for Medicare, her 3 sons were finally grown and out of the house, my business was doing better, and we had started tithing.

Eventually, several of Betty's doctors agreed that she needed to be committed to The Pavilion because they suspected she had a prescription drug addiction. We agreed to go along with what they suggested, and Betty gave them 6 weeks of her life but none of her cooperation. It was no surprise it proved futile. Soon after that, an oral surgeon diagnosed her with TMJ, and she went to Montgomery, Alabama, for surgery on one side of her jaw. A year later, Betty returned for surgery on the other side, and it cured her headaches.

In 1998, Betty developed a staph infection from her last hernia surgery. After an unsuccessful year of fighting the staph infection, we couldn't find a surgeon in Amarillo who would touch her except Dr. Dove at the Texas Tech University Medical Center. He said the infection was in the fiberglass mesh used in her abdomen to prevent the hernia from erupting again. After the surgery to remove the mesh, Betty was rushed from recovery to ICU because she couldn't breathe on her own. She spent 22 days on a ventilator in ICU. Twice they tried to take her off. The first time lasted an hour-and-a-half, and the second time was for 18 hours. The doctors informed me after 20 days, a ventilator tube does more harm than good. All Betty's surgeons agreed she needed to be sent home with a tracheotomy tube and live the rest of her life on a ventilator.

Dr. Sahad, her pulmonologist, talked the surgeon into giving him the weekend to get Betty off the ventilator before they put in a permanent tracheotomy tube.

He called me Sunday night and said, "God willing, I'm going to remove the tube at 9 a.m. Monday morning." And he did.

With the mesh gone and the staph cleared up, Betty regained a certain degree of health after returning home. Eventually she developed hard lung, where the lungs no longer expand and retract. In 2003, she began sleeping with oxygen. By 2004, she was dependent on oxygen 24/7 for the last 5 years of her life.

DYING MOMENTS

Unexplainable and Irreversible

It was March 2006. Betty called me at the office to come home and drive her to the beauty shop. Normally she drove herself. When I got to the house, I went in the kitchen and told her I was ready to take her.

She said, "I'm not going."

That made no sense so I asked her if she'd changed her mind about getting her hair fixed, but her only reply was, "I'm not going."

I asked her what was wrong and she said nothing was wrong, she was fine. She told me to go back to work, but I stayed home so I could keep an eye on her.

The next morning, she wanted to lie in the guest bedroom so she could look out the window onto the street. I got her comfortable and went to work. When I came home, she was exactly as I left her. I realized she'd stopped eating, drinking, and taking her medications. Several of her prescriptions were to be weaned off gradually if her doctors ever decided to take her off, but she stopped them all in a single day. Betty never again took an aspirin, antacid, or had another drink of alcohol.

From that moment, I was desperate for answers and for someone to help us, so I pushed and pushed. Everyone in the family; sons, grandson, and sisters-in-law, took their turn trying to get Betty to take her meds and eat. Leticia ran Good Care Services which took care of the elderly, and Donna was a hospice volunteer-coordinator. Both of my sisters came to the house and tried to reason with Betty. Donna even tried to trick Betty by mashing up some of her medications, blending them in oatmeal, and spoon-feeding her.

Betty took one bite and told Donna, "Are you trying to spoon feed me like a baby? Don't you understand? I don't want this!"

I contacted our cardiologist, Dr. Soya. I trusted him. I thought he could tell me what to do with Betty. Surely, someone could do something to help her.

Finally he'd had enough, and he bluntly told me, "You need to face reality, Ron. Your wife is dying. I've seen this hundreds of times. Betty's in the dying process. I don't know how long it will be, but she's dying."

Those words slapped me in the face and brought me to reality. Though Betty had come back from horrible problems time after time, she was never going to recover from this. She was dying, really dying. Dr. Soya signed the papers to enroll her in in-home hospice.

All of us had been tiptoeing around and talking about her condition in whispers outside of her room. Finally, I came right out and asked her point blank, "Do you want to die?"

She emphatically answered, "NO!"

That's when I told her she could go without eating and without medications for a little while but if she went without water for more than 5 days, she'd dehydrate, her kidneys would shut down, there would be no reversal, and she would die. So she started drinking water, but she didn't eat for the next 6 weeks. It was so hard to believe that people always jumped to the conclusion she was probably eating when no one was watching. I know she didn't eat. We were all so anxious for a sign that she was getting better that we kept a close eye on her as well as all the food in the house. We had a sunken living room, and she couldn't walk into the kitchen and step up without help. I'm positive that she didn't eat. Finally after 60 days, she thought she might like to try a piece of toast with water. Betty was 4-foot-11, and she'd gone down from 125 pounds to only 70.

For the rest of her life she stayed at 70 pounds and only ate 2 meals a day. At first, she ate a light breakfast of one scrambled egg and one slice of toast. In the middle of the afternoon she had soup. By her last year, she graduated to eating a child-size hamburger from Wendy's.

This was a total about face for Betty. She loved to eat, and when we traveled she never concerned herself with any aspect of our trip except finding some place special and different to eat. When we checked in for the night, without fail she asked the desk clerk, "Where's the best place in town to eat?"

Betty was in hospice for 3 years. She was frail and she mainly went from our bed, to the bathroom, and to her recliner. Even standing up and making those small journeys required someone by her side. Hard lung didn't allow Betty to take a deep breath, so the slightest exertion wore her out.

After months and months of this I was going stir crazy, and I couldn't understand how she could stand it. I'd tell her about the things happening outside our house, trying to pique her curiosity. I hoped she would *want* to go outside and see something. I frequently asked to put her in the car and simply take her for a ride. I told her she could put on her robe and sunglasses and no one would pay any attention to her riding in our car. Instead of saying a flat "no" she always said "maybe tomorrow". It never happened. She refused to sit with me on our patio. I could hardly get her to stand at the front door with me and look outside at the snow or the leaves changing color.

Betty always loved clothes and shopping, but after that pivotal day she stayed in nightgowns. Debbie bought Betty clothes for her birthday because none of her old clothes would have fit her since she'd lost half her body weight. After she opened the package and looked at the new clothes, she asked Elberta to put them in the closet. I found the box and the clothes with the tags still on them in her side of the closet when I had our estate sale. Betty left the house only once in those 3 years. She went to the high school graduation party for our twin niece and nephew, Audra and Aaron, at Leticia's house.

Betty's health insurance was unobtainable until the latter years, and then it was unaffordable. It wasn't until the last 5 years of her life that she qualified for Medicare that we made a dent in her medical debt. It seemed ironic that she had a 2-page list of medications, but after she got on Medicare, she took herself off all her medications for the last 3 years of her life.

An Army of 2 😊

I own and operate Mid-West Glove and Supply. After the first day Betty stayed home, I never felt safe leaving her alone anymore. On the second day, I had no idea what I was up against and that this was only the beginning. Betty steadily deteriorated for 6 weeks, and then stayed the same for the next 3 years.

Donna knew a hospice worker who she felt would be ideal for everything Betty and I needed. Elberta came and got down on her knee beside Betty's chair and told her how much she wanted to come and help out until she started feeling better. Betty told Elberta she didn't need her help and asked her to leave. I was ashamed that Betty was so ugly to her. Elberta looked up at me, and I just shrugged. So she told Betty she came because I had called her and she was going to stay.

I was Betty's caregiver on weekends, in the mornings before Elberta arrived, and again in the evenings. For me, living life was replaced by a grinding determination to merely exist. I thank God for Elberta Turner! She joined me, and we became an army of 2. She was the loyal and dear friend Betty and I needed so badly. Because Elberta was so reliable, I was able to focus on running the business while I was at work.

In 2008 I had a knee replacement, and when I came home from the hospital, Elberta had 2 invalids to care for. She packed my knee in ice before she left in the afternoon and returned before bedtime to do it again. She also drove me to my doctor's appointments and my physical therapy.

In the meantime, her husband retired from Pantex and moved to south Texas to build their dream house. Elberta stayed in their empty house and slept on a mattress on the floor. On weekends, she was at her home in a house without furniture or her husband so she could continue to help out with Betty. Elberta told me she wanted to stay with Betty for as long as she lived. Finally, her house was complete, and she had to pack up what little she still had in their Amarillo house and leave. Elberta had been coming to my house 5 days a week without a vacation for more than 3 years. When Elberta gave notice that she would be leaving us in another week, I got busy and found a replacement. I told the new lady to come to the house at 10 a.m. Monday morning, July 6, 2009. That Friday was Elberta's last day, and she said her goodbyes.

That Sunday evening, I helped Betty to the bathroom before we went to bed. After I'd settle her, she always insisted that I leave the bathroom. She claimed she had a shy bladder and could never go if I was close enough to hear her. So as usual I waited right outside the door for her to call me back in. When she didn't call me, I called to her. She didn't answer, so I went back in to help her up.

She had passed out and was slumped over. I carried her to our bed and called the hospice nurse and Donna. They came over, but there really wasn't anything we could do for Betty. The nurse said it wasn't unusual for this to happen several times before someone died. Betty eventually opened her eyes and seemed to remember nothing.

The next morning, everything seemed completely normal. Betty sat on the edge of the bed, and we talked as usual. She said she needed to go to the bathroom but hated to in case what happened the night before happened again. Eventually she couldn't wait any longer. I helped her, but again, she passed out and again, I laid her on our bed and called the hospice nurse. Next, I called my office and told Russ I'd be a little late coming in. When I got off the phone and looked at Betty, she was gone.

Elberta hadn't left town yet and when she heard the news, she came right back to my house to help. Pastor Jay called the new lady who was to start that morning and explained that her services would not be needed after all. Elberta accomplished her goal. She had stayed with Betty all the way to the end. I think Elberta and Betty liked it better that way. I know I did.

Always On Call 😊

In addition to being a caregiver, I washed laundry, cleaned house, and cooked meals. If I needed to go to the bank, grocery, or dry cleaner, I could only be gone for little more than an hour. Betty couldn't get to the bathroom by herself, and she'd had a weak bladder since she was 40-years-old. Even when she was healthy, on a 130-mile trip with our nephews from Portales to our house, Betty had to stop 3 or 4 times. Those little guys, Greg and Russ, nicknamed her Aunt Betsy Wetsie and Betty was a good sport about it.

In the beginning, she absolutely refused to have a bathroom chair set beside her bed or recliner while I was away. And no pull-ups for her! Near the very end when she had to get up several times a night to urinate she did finally allow the chair. Before the chair, there were times that I was at the grocery store with a basket full of groceries, some of it frozen or refrigerated, and she'd call on my cell and insist that I stop and come home that instant. I soon got in the habit of buying the frozen foods last. Whether I was mowing or running errands, when I got her call, I had to drop everything and run home to help her to the bathroom.

Betty had always been a movie fanatic, and she called every day for me to pick up a movie on my way home. I hated looking for videos with a passion! I really needed that time for errands or grocery shopping. We'd watch even the most horrible movies until at least 10 p.m. and then switch to the news followed by *The Tonight Show*. When I couldn't take it any longer, I'd get on my computer to escape. When she was ready for bed, she called me to walk her to the bedroom. She always wanted me to go to bed at the same time she did. Some nights I would, but some nights I just couldn't.

Eventually, I would have to go to bed. How I dreaded the heat! Betty was always cold because she wasn't active and was so thin. Our bedroom was sweltering but she insisted the ceiling fan could cause a draft and she'd catch pneumonia. I'd lie on top of the covers and stare up at our ceiling fan, wishing for the slightest breeze.

The other problem was the TV. Betty slept late and dozed off and on all during the day. She insisted on having the TV on until she fell asleep. If I turned it off and got into bed without waking her, all was well. But if I turned it off and she wasn't sound asleep or if it woke her up, she would wait a few minutes until she decided I'd had a reasonable amount of time to fall asleep, and then she'd turn the TV back on.

However, most of the time I was *almost asleep*, so it would wake me back up and I'd say, "Betty, what are you doing?"

Her reply was always the same, "You know I can't go to sleep without noise. If I get back to sleep, *then* you can turn it off."

I would have gone into one of our other bedrooms, but she insisted she needed me close during the night. Since I could hear her call from the living room, most of the nights that I couldn't sleep I opted for my recliner.

A Brief Encounter Made a Vital Difference

In 2008, I had my second total knee replacement. An anesthesiologist came into the holding room to meet me and explain his part of the procedure. He said he would see me in the surgery room, and he left. Soon he returned.

His first words were, "I know you don't know me. And I certainly don't want to offend you. But I was having my coffee and I couldn't get you off of my mind. I want to ask you a question, but please don't be offended. How many people do you know your size that's 70 years old or older?"

I told him I'd need to think about it.

Even after I was home, I frequently thought about his question but I could never come up with one single person. But even though I wanted to do something about my weight, I had 2 strikes against me. First, I had a wife who wanted me to sit and watch movies with her every single night. Second, I was too depressed to make any changes in my life even if I'd had plenty of time.

About a year after Betty died, I started water aerobics, and 3 months later I started to diet. It was 8 months later that I joined Christian Mingle, and by that time I had lost 80 pounds. k was right when she said she could tell from the way I held the bottom of my sweater close to my stomach that I had just lost weight and that I was proud of it.

The 800-pound Gorilla 😊

Betty didn't like to talk about dying. Only once, years before while standing in church, she had nudged me while we were singing and said, "That's the song I want sung at my funeral." When we sat down, I flipped my Bible open to the front cover and copied the name of the song from the church bulletin. At that time, Betty was healthy. When we were making her funeral plans, that song was the only funeral request Betty had made. I had to go to the top of my closet and search through the inside covers of all my old Bibles to find the name of the song.

From the day she stopped taking all of her medications, eating, and drinking until she died 3 years later, Betty always maintained that she didn't need to be in hospice, she didn't need Elberta, and she wasn't dying. She bellyached and complained that all the visits from hospice nurses, caregivers, spiritual counselors, bereavement counselors, and doctors were all a big waste of time and money. She lived the biggest life of denial anyone could imagine. Her continued existence became a way of life. Though all the medical professionals insisted she was dying, I never once considered that I'd walk into the room and find her dead. Day after day, month after month, and year after year I came home, and she was still sitting in her chair very much alive!

The morning Betty died, I called the hospice nurse, went into the sunroom to sit, and waited for someone to arrive. The oxygenator was still running. It was loud. I looked over at the machine and realized there was no longer a need for it to keep running. So

I walked over and turned it off. For the first time in 3 years, there was total silence. I hadn't experienced it in such a long time. Medical professionals had said Betty was dying. Betty had insisted that she wasn't dying. The silence of the oxygenator settled the dispute.

Sitting in my usual chair, I picked up my Bible out of habit and it came to my mind that I could read the twenty-third Psalms. I read them out loud and thought about what it meant to me at that moment. While I was sitting there and coming to grips with the situation, my doorbell rang. First the hospice nurse, next Donna, then other family and friends arrived. Before long, the house was full. It was as if Betty had simply gone to sleep. Her death was easy and without any signs of struggle. The weight of the responsibility for Betty had started to lift with the shutting off of the oxygenator, and my life was transitioning naturally. The 800-pound gorilla had left the room. I had no regrets because I had loved her and shown my love right up until her very last breath. I refused to let myself feel guilty because I felt relieved from the responsibility of taking care of Betty. We'd both lived in constant struggle for years, and now neither of us had to struggle any more.

St. Patrick's Day 2006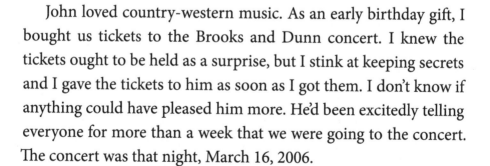

John loved country-western music. As an early birthday gift, I bought us tickets to the Brooks and Dunn concert. I knew the tickets ought to be held as a surprise, but I stink at keeping secrets and I gave the tickets to him as soon as I got them. I don't know if anything could have pleased him more. He'd been excitedly telling everyone for more than a week that we were going to the concert. The concert was that night, March 16, 2006.

The last conversation we had was the morning of his wreck. I always did the yard work, but I'd been out of town with Evelyn and

Kori, John's sister and niece, shopping for a prom dress. While I was away, John mowed. I wanted to be sure he knew I appreciated his help. I hoped if he ever retired, maybe he'd help with the yard. John was backing out of our driveway, so I hurried to catch him. I knocked on the pickup hood and motioned for him to roll down the passenger window so he could hear me. When I thanked him, he told me he didn't run the weed-eater or edge. I told him it didn't matter; I really appreciated that he mowed at all. He smiled and told me I'd better appreciate it. Then he rolled up the window, and he was gone.

Deb and I had started meeting for coffee on Thursday mornings more than 25 years ago, and it became a weekly social event for us and all of our friends. That was a Thursday morning, so I headed out for coffee as usual. The table was full, and everyone was talkative. Courtney came in a little late after dropping her kids off at elementary school. She was disgusted! She'd managed to be the radio listener who got through to answer the question that would win Brooks and Dunn concert tickets. She knew the correct answer but in all her excitement, she gave the wrong answer. She couldn't believe it. I didn't have the heart to tell her I had 2 concert tickets with me.

After coffee, Doris and I went to exercise at Curves. We'd just arrived when my cell phone rang. It was Justin.

"Mom, Dad's been hit by a train. Bring all his medications and meet the ambulance at the hospital."

I like to tell myself that I'm not the type to panic and that I usually wait and listen to hear all the details. As I listened I thought, *Maybe the train hit the bumper. Maybe the pickup rolled over. He might have cuts and bruises and nothing more.*

My legs gave way and I literally fell to my knees on the floor when he finished with, "Life Star will meet us there and they'll airlift him to the trauma center in Amarillo." In my heart I knew this was it.

Doris offered to ride with me, but I told her, "No, I'll be alright."

All the way home I talked to myself. "Stay calm. Don't panic. It'll be okay. You won't be any help if you fall apart now. Just think positive." At least I didn't have to struggle to keep from crying. Nothing seemed real. As I drove down the familiar streets to my house, it was a beautiful spring day. Surely if this were actually happening, the weather wouldn't be so beautiful and the morning so peaceful and still.

When I got to the hospital, I was amazed to see so many friends already there waiting. I fumbled as I searched for John's insurance card in my wallet, but I simply couldn't find it. My friend sitting next to me asked if she could help. She reached into my jumble of cards and instantly picked out the correct insurance card. That's when I realized I was only kidding myself. I wasn't cool, and I wasn't calm.

It seemed to take forever as we waited for the ambulance to arrive. When it finally did, they ushered me in to speak to John before they loaded him into the helicopter. I recognized his coat but not John. He was swollen, and his glasses were missing. I saw no wounds or blood. His clothes weren't even torn. I took hold of his puffy hand and told him not to worry, everything was going to be alright, and he was in good hands.

When I asked the nurse at the emergency room if I should run back home and pack a bag before I left, she said, "Just GO!"

She was certainly right. Justin drove me. That was back when it was legal to talk on a cell phone while driving. Justin did both.

There were even more friends at the trauma center when we arrived in Amarillo. We were all moved out of the main emergency waiting area and squeezed into a tiny family room. Most of the people were visiting in hushed tones, and that was fine. But it was all the people talking on their cell phones that about killed me. I wanted to scream, "Take those phones outside!" Justin must have been struggling too. He left. When I saw him next, he was by himself with his head down low in the neck of his coat. I wished I'd thought of that. I understood how he felt. I wanted to hide too.

One person I was especially glad to see was Courtney. She had cut John's hair for a long time, and they were both big fans of country-western music. Just 2 hours earlier, she'd been upset because she'd missed her chance to win Brooks and Dunn concert tickets. If she hadn't talked about it at coffee I wouldn't have thought to give her the tickets that I still had in my purse. I would have hated it when I found them unused later on. Instead, it was perfect. John loved Courtney, and he would have been glad his tickets went to her.

Eventually the parade of doctors began. The first doctor said he was surprised John had brain waves, and they were going to do exploratory surgery and try to stop the bleeding. They told me to follow behind his gurney to surgery. The nurses pushing his bed were laughing and talking as if we were going to a ball game. I was overwhelmed. I desperately needed to feel the hospital staff was concerned professionals but I did not! I was left in a waiting area by myself, and the nurse handed me John's wedding ring. I was falling apart. This was real. There was no one but me.

My sister and Mel both called and offered to come. I asked them not to. I felt if they flew in, I would be responsible for transportation, meals, and lodging for them, and I didn't even know what I was going to do with myself at that point. Right then, the idea of out-of-town company was too much for me to handle.

Catching Rain with a Fork

I had a horrible time trying to understand all that each specialist explained. I listened desperately, but I felt helpless to retain the information. It was like trying to catch rain with a fork. Each time the doors opened, in came a different doctor with more news, different news, different evaluations, and nothing ever seemed to fit together. It was obvious that none of the doctors had conferred. By evening, I was worn out from trying to comprehend and retain all their information.

From the look of the pickup, the train had hit in the center of the driver's door and pushed it down the track until it rolled off the rails and down the incline on the right side. John was thrown out of the pickup. It landed upside down and on top of him. The weight of the pickup was held up by the roof of the cab, and that's why he wasn't crushed. His left leg and arm were both broken. All of his ribs on the left side were broken as well as several of the ribs on his right side. Both lungs were punctured. His pelvis was crushed. His neck was broken at the second vertebra, but the spinal cord wasn't severed. He had internal bleeding. There was a tear in his bladder, and his spleen had ruptured.

According to the doctors, all of that was fixable. The entire medical staff talked very reassuringly to us. Even though I'd believed from the first mention of the helicopter that John wouldn't survive, I slowly began to doubt my initial assumption. Maybe he would survive after all.

Some of my children were with me, and we were going home to Dumas. We needed to regroup, pack, and return in the morning–fresh and with a plan.

It had been a long day. Less than 18 hours earlier, I thanked John in our driveway for mowing the lawn. That last conversation felt so long ago.

Before we reached the city limits of Amarillo, the hospital called and we hurried straight back. The verdict was the worst. His brain had begun to swell. They had immediately removed part of his skull but still the pressure continued to mount. In a matter of hours, his pressure had reached such a high level that the doctor said his recovery was impossible.

Right on the heels of that news was a request for John to be an organ donor. I agreed because Janice's daughter needed a kidney. Thanks to Candice, I had a face and a life attached to the idea of John being an organ donor. After I agreed, I spent the rest of the night filling out the required forms for John to qualify. As I answered endless questions about his medical history, I realized how young and healthy he truly was. If it wasn't for the train wreck, it seemed he might have lived forever. John was only 58. At the time I'm writing this, his father is 90, still lives at home by himself, and drives.

The next morning, we drove back to Amarillo. The doctor said it wouldn't be much longer. I asked the nurses to remove his neck brace, ventilator tube, the wire probes coming out of his skull, and everything else so we could see him and say goodbye. I had hoped that John would look more like himself after everything was taken away. But he didn't.

My Burning Bush Experience

John's small ICU room was full of family. I said my goodbye to him first, and then I left the room so others could say their good-byes in private. I went to the empty ICU waiting room by myself. I was so angry because I was completely helpless. I was just about to tell God, "I will never love another man and no other man will ever touch me for as long as I live!" but I remembered hearing that you shouldn't make a vow during a moment of intense emotion. People often change their minds, regret what they said, and want to take it back. But God takes a vow seriously! Though I had only been a widow a few minutes, I already hated it! Why say something needlessly that might prevent my life from ever moving off this spot? I threw on the brakes and stopped myself from issuing that vow.

Instead of me telling God what I would not do, I heard Him tell me what He would do. A totally illogical thought came welling up inside of me. *The end will be better than the beginning.*

I was stunned! I didn't deserve anything good. I felt my subconscious had created that thought to comfort me.

I didn't know it then, but I was headed into the 5 worst years of my life. It was especially during those horrible times that I hated myself for clinging to a stupid, illogical belief that God had actually spoken to my heart and promised me that the end would be better than the beginning. But it was my only hope, and my heart simply wouldn't give it up. So I told no one and tried not to think about it too often.

Little did I know, March, 2006 was also a pivotal year for a man whose wife had just stopped eating, taking her medications, getting dressed, or leaving their house. Ron and I had no way of knowing we were both entering the valley of the shadow of death at the same time and would also emerge at the same time. We had lived, and we would continue to live completely different lives... for now.

Forced to Decide ALONE

I remember one of our few morning conversations only 2 or 3

months before the wreck. John was in his typical rush. While he was dressing, I tried to get him to make at least one decision about a cemetery or our funerals. I'd been disappointed when he said he didn't want us to be buried at the little country cemetery in Sunray. Predictably, John became exasperated when I pushed for a decision on a subject he was never in the mood to discuss anyway.

I told him, "Please, don't leave the house without deciding on at least one issue this morning."

He whirled around, looked at me, and said, "Just cremate me," then he walked briskly out of the room.

I thought that conversation was another failure. Cremation wasn't what he wanted. What he really wanted was for me to get off his back. With cremation, the subject was closed. No cemetery, head stone, inscription, mortuary, open or closed casket, visitation night, or pallbearers. So, I just shelved the subject knowing there would be another day, a better day, when we could calmly discuss and make these decisions together without pressure. But I was wrong.

John was so swollen after the train wreck, and with part of his skull removed he was unrecognizable. If he had looked like himself, I don't know that I could have gone through with the cremation. He had never wanted to be inconvenienced with a discussion on the unpleasant topic of funeral planning. A few months earlier when he was under no pressures, he refused to make even one decision about our funerals. I'd just turned off his ventilator, and I was an emotional wreck. How was I supposed to make funeral decisions now, by myself? I had nothing left in me. He owed me his help. This was a couple's decision. Because of 36 years of avoidance, he'd abandoned me in my hour of need. I wonder what he'd have done if I had died first. If he was in the same emotional condition I was in, could he have started firing off answers and making decisions on behalf of the 2 of us? Of course not.

I took his flippant answer of cremation as my release from agonizing over the decisions any further.

Déjà vu 😊

John's family was present when I made the decision to turn off life support, and I said he'd be cremated. I looked around the room and asked if there were any objections. I praise God that no one argued even though it must have been shocking. No one knew about our last conversation about funerals. Looking back, I don't know why I did most of the stuff I did. If I had to do it over again, I'm not sure I'd do it all the same or if I'd make changes. I try not to second guess myself on this.

Our family was in a similar situation 3 years later with my youngest son. After Adam's ATV accident, it was my daughter-in-law's turn to make all those same decisions including the decision to turn off the life support. Becca had the added responsibility of their 2-year-old daughter, Acie, to take into consideration.

I was so grateful that I didn't have to decide for my son. Even after 3 years, I had no additional insight or better answers. I respected Becca for the way she shouldered the heavy responsibility. I tried to be as supportive of her as everyone had been for me.

Standing Room Only 😊

We had been members of Calvary for 35 years so we wanted John's funeral service held there. We decided, since the sanctuary was small, to have a public funeral at 1 p.m. and a second, more informal service for our church family at 6 p.m. The weather was bitter cold with snow, but still the church was packed. People were standing in the back and crowded into the side aisles. There was a line of people waiting in the hallway who never got to go inside the sanctuary. I'm proud so many people came to honor John at both services. I knew John genuinely loved people. I just didn't know that they loved him back.

At the second service, people were invited to come forward and say whatever was in their hearts. Many did. Our family heard wonderful things about John that we would not have learned any other way. It was a great day for our entire family and for John.

Merely Existing After Death

It Was ALL Hard 💗

I didn't have the energy to make small talk with Good Samaritans who were out doing their 'good deed' for the day. I didn't want to be someone's project. Granted, I was lonely, but that wasn't the answer I was looking for. Being grateful was the only thing that ever helped me overcome my sadness. I would recall all there was to be grateful for; John was a Christian, he raised all 3 of his children to be adults, he had taught his sons to make a living in agriculture, and he lived long enough to see 6 little grandsons born. The more blessings I named, the more came to mind.

Our crops were completely wiped out by hail 2 years out of 3. There were 2 full years of business and personal expenses with hardly any income. Still, our local bank continued to loan us capital so we could stay in business. Recounting the good memories would eventually lift the heaviness, and I could stop crying and get up off the floor.

Keeping a grateful attitude was similar to a decision to eat healthy. It wasn't a one-time decision, but one that had to be repeated often. I made the initial decision to be grateful, but I had to recall my blessings every time self-pity and loneliness smothered me. Sometimes I did it right, but honestly, many times over the next 5 years, I didn't. In public I thought I was doing a good job of smiling, but at home I was nobody's hero. I struggled with anger, depression, and self-pity. My down times ranged from a few hours to weeks or even months. The only way out of the pit was to take hold of gratitude and pull myself out.

Genuine, heartfelt gratitude is a powerful emotion, but mere lip service is too watered-down to overcome depression. It was especially difficult for me to shake myself and stand up tall as long as people were lavishing me with their sympathy and pity. Too much comforting from family and friends eventually creates a trap for the bereaved.

What's the Point?

The one bit of advice I heard repeatedly was, "They say to wait a year before you make any major changes."

As soon as people delivered this piece of advice, they would turn around and return to their normal lives with their families. I was supposed to be satisfied to sit patiently and do nothing until a year passed. No one ever explained to me what the benefits of waiting a year would be. Was something good going to *suddenly* happen the way toast pops up out of a toaster? In a year, would I magically be better prepared to make decisions? Would the opportunities I missed out on during my year of waiting recycle back around and give me a second chance?

I think the point of waiting a year was for loneliness to become a person's new normal. Once comfortable, why would anyone want to uproot **AGAIN** for any reason? The bereaved can snuggle down in quiet solitude until it hardens like cement.

Filling the Void

Won't Somebody Please Live with Me!

To take my mind off my loneliness, I invited both of my single friends to live with me. I owned a duplex and suggested to Doris, my widowed friend from church, that we sell our large family homes and move in together. We could get out from under expenses and responsibilities to enjoy our lives and travel. I was strong enough to lift her wheelchair, and she was still healthy enough to enjoy traveling.

I told her, "You say that you want to go to Switzerland. There will never be a better time than now. Let's go! Someday we'll regret it if we don't. We have the money, the time, and a traveling companion. We can do this, Doris. Please do this with me!"

But she refused.

Mel, my friend from my school days, lived in Waco and had retired because of her vision. Her house was a lot for her to maintain but, even so, she also refused to move in with me. How much lower could my life get?

My New Husband was a Dog

What was I to do? Get a dog? Okay, if that was my only option, I would. At 55, I got my first dog. He was a hand-me-down from a friend who was trying to find him a new home. I named him Husband because a *husband* was what I really wanted.

The first morning at my house, Husband tried to roust me out of bed at about 5:30 a.m. I informed him that I didn't operate like that. Lying in bed was my favorite escape from facing the blues. It wasn't illegal, immoral, fattening, expensive, and it didn't require a partner. Besides, I didn't have any place to go, and no one was counting on me for anything. Husband was difficult, moody, and bossy in a silent sort of way. He didn't like any of the dog foods or treats I bought him except when I first opened the bag and the aroma was the strongest. After that, the little snob turned his nose up. He didn't like me to pet or hold him. It seemed I could never please him regardless of what I did.

I filled my lonely days and evenings walking my dog, playing Sudoku on my phone, and taking Tylenol PM in the evenings so I could read a book and go to bed early. Life was empty, and so was I. There was no relief in sight.

John died on St. Patrick's Day. Adam died on the 4th of July, and Husband was run over on Veteran's Day. He hopped out of the car when I stopped to get gas. I drove around Sunray looking for him and found him dead in the middle of Main Street. It must have just happened because when I picked him up, he drew his last breath, made one little quiver, and he was gone. It was very emotional – John, my son, and my life that I loved were all gone, and I didn't even get to keep *the dog*! There are moments of heart-break and self-pity that are perfect for a good long cry, and that was a doozey!

I didn't know what to do with a dead dog, so I drove out to the farm and asked my 8-year-old grandson, Connor, to help me. He had buried his dogs, and I asked him to bury mine.

Out of the Frying Pan and into the Fire

I had stayed in Arlington for 6 months during the end of my

daughter's pregnancy with her twins, Chaz and Kason. I was there to help out with Jadan, 4, and Gage, 2. After John died, whenever I went to my daughter's, I felt at home. I squeezed in at the dinner table, called dibs on the front passenger seat in the van, gave baths, and changed diapers. I was terrific at running the dishwasher, and when it came to doing laundry, I was a machine. Some days I took a nap. All the other days I took 2.

There were times it was sensory overload to be around an active young family with 4 bouncing boys. Jagee and Larry Dan were generous to allow me easy access into their lives, but I could only cope if I did it one day at a time. I went to their house to get away from the silence and from feeling totally useless. Then, I went home before I cracked up. Their house was a wonderful place to visit, but I wasn't man enough to live there full-time. Sometimes I thought that perhaps her young family was grateful to see me come, but they might be even more grateful to see me go.

Is Green Acres the Place for Me?

When our sons were big enough to work on the farm, I phased out. I got to pursue my dream of becoming a wedding photographer. Eventually I got the opportunity to be a partner in a remodeling business. I enjoyed both jobs for about 10 years each. I was retired and writing a short weekly column for our local newspaper, but when John died, I stopped writing as well.

Justin was farming with John, and Stephanie was doing the paperwork before John died. Many people asked me, confidentially and in hushed tones, if I thought Justin would be able to "keep things afloat" with John gone. It never occurred to me that he might not. Justin and Steph might be young, but they are smart, and they work hard. Adam and Becca joined our operation and the 5 of us became Lone Star Family Farms in January 2009. Adam was killed in a wreck 7 months later, but Becca has stayed involved with LSFF.

Without John, I was living in my dream home, my adult children were making a good living for me, and I didn't have a care in the world...*or a purpose.*

Justin issued a standing invitation for me to bring a bottle of water and a book and ride in the pickup or tractor with him from sun up to sun down. He promised to find things for me to do even if he had to invent them, which he frequently did. He even let me plow weeds – in our oldest tractor of course!

Eventually I got a promotion, and I was driving our farm equipment into the John Deere dealership for repairs and for trade-ins. I also brought the new equipment back out to the barn. It was about a 20-mile jaunt through the country if I took the back roads. Once, I drove a new combine into an electric pole and it wrapped the ladder around the tire. My sons gave me some time off. Finally they cooled down and allowed me to return to work, and I was given my choice of jobs. I could run the broom or the hoe.

Justin's family was good to include me, but even being included was hard. I never knew where to sit in the suburban or at the dinner table or where to position myself among them when we walked across a parking lot. I worried that I'd be intruding if I sat between Justin and Steph. Was my place between Cole and Connor or should I sit between the parent and the child? They never acted as if it was a problem for them, but it was a big problem for me. My place was beside John, and he wasn't around anymore.

Justin and Stephanie were building a house on the farm. One night, I called Justin with a brilliant idea! I could sell my brand new house and divide the money 3 ways for my kids to pay toward their houses, and then I could rotate staying with each of my children. Justin was silent for such a long time that I thought we'd been disconnected, and then he said, "Mom, don't you want my marriage to work?" He was right. I really only wanted one thing more than to be included and that was for my adult children to have happy, healthy families. I wanted my grandchildren to see me as something other than a tag-along. Still, I wanted to be included in everything the kids did and I certainly didn't keep it a secret. Stephanie was amazing! She generously included me in family vacations and holiday celebrations. I think she saved my life.

The Single Life Loses its Luster

In the Gillespie family, deaths always follow lengthy illnesses. People never die suddenly. You would suppose I should have been somewhat prepared, but even after 3 years in hospice, the realization arrived abruptly. At first, there was the sense of relief when the pressure of caring for Betty was immediately and completely gone.

Please don't misunderstand; I never wanted Betty to die. I'm saying I never thought of what my life would be like without the responsibility of her. I merely kept my head down and pushed with all my strength for both of us to survive. But once Betty was actually gone, I was glad for Betty. She was finally free from her struggles.

Amazingly, the 800-pound gorilla was lifted from my shoulders when my years of care-giving duty came to a close. I was now responsible for just myself. I distinctly remember thinking, *I don't care if I ever have anyone in my life to be responsible for again.* Hopefully you can understand what it was like for me to be free to live and do as I wanted. In that *one* respect life was good. Life was great! I decided, "I can do this forever. It won't bother me to be on my own from now on!"

The joy of a carefree lifestyle was short-lived. I eventually realized I hadn't enjoyed being single after my divorce from my first wife when I was a young man, and I didn't like it one bit better as a senior. That glorious freedom was only good at work and play, or when I was doing things with other people. The rest of the time I wasn't free, I was alone. I found it a little less lonely to stay in my empty office at work after everyone went home than to go to my house. Whether I was at home or at work, I killed time shopping for collector's knives and Betty Boop memorabilia on eBay.

Eating out lost its appeal. Everywhere I looked there were couples and families, and I felt even more alone. I started calling my orders in and getting my meals as takeout. It was strange because I'd been a salesman for more than 8 years eating breakfast, lunch, and dinner alone, out on the road 3 or 4 days each week. But it was entirely different back then because I knew it was temporary, and I'd soon be home with my family. It was sobering to know that eating alone was my new lifestyle. I dreaded going home to a big, empty, silent house. As much as I had grown to hate TV, I turned it on for background noise because I couldn't take the quiet!

The next thing I knew, I was intentionally looking for ways to include myself in the lives of my family. To offset my guilt for crowding into their family time, I would gladly pick up the tab regardless of the cost. I just wanted to be with someone. I'd go to their house, eat with small, sticky children, watch a movie, and take their families out to eat or buy theater tickets. I'd do absolutely anything to keep from going home. But I couldn't impose forever. Eventually I had to face the fact that they had their own lives to lead. It was at that point I began to think it wouldn't be so bad to find a nice lady after all. We could go to the movies or out to eat, anything to fill that void. At least I'd be doing my family a favor.

We're Getting Warmer

Finding the Woman of my Dreams Might Be the Same as a Snipe Hunt

Thoughts of finding a lady friend continued to grow, but I wanted to be cautious and smart. I wasn't about to go to a night-club or lounge to meet a woman. I knew that wasn't what I wanted. In fact, I still wanted the type of woman that I had always wanted. I wanted the nice girl next door, but I doubted there were any of those left.

One thing I knew for certain, I wouldn't be happy with a woman if she wasn't a Christian. I heeded my pastor's advice and depended totally on God to be my source. I started concluding my daily devotional with prayer, acknowledging God as my only hope of finding the right woman to date and possibly develop a relationship with. If God wasn't at the forefront of her life, I wasn't interested in her as a friend or a wife!

There was a woman where I exercised who had a new story every Monday morning about the different men she met and took home for the weekend. She offered to meet me for coffee or have me over to her place to watch a movie. Her invitation was pretty blatant. But that wasn't for me. It felt good to be put to the test and pass!

I was very close to finding k and turning my life around, but I had no way of knowing it at the time. What I'd always wanted was very near, and all I had to do was stay on course.

One night, I got on my computer and typed "Christian dating for free" in the search bar. There was far too much information and some of it was really shocking. By the end of the evening, I decided my idea was a bad one and abandoned the idea of online dating.

Climbing a Barbed Wire Fence Naked

A few months after John died, I wrote this list of husband qualifications. Almost 5 years later, I would meet the man who was exactly what I was looking for.

Man of integrity who loves God first and family second.

Crazy about me (loves, respects, and admires me, and vice versa).

Encourages me to write. Knows enough to give me analytical advice for my writing but not so educated that he's bored and critical of the things I write.

Reasonable and decisive.

Not in debt.

Lives in the Panhandle.

Has some free time.

He has places to go and allows me the same freedom.

He knows, "She's the girl for me."

*He would **gladly** climb a barbed wire fence **naked** if that's what it took to win me.*

He will say sweet things to me like, "I love you. You're beautiful."

Christian Mingle

A Safe Place to Begin 😊

Like the rest of America, I was recording my favorite programs on DVR so I could watch them without commercials. One evening, I got busy during a show and suddenly became aware that the commercials were on. As I picked up the remote to fast-forward, a commercial for Christian Mingle (CM) came on. I immediately wrote down their web address. When I went online I had total freedom to surf their website, and I could clearly see they were protecting their members' identities and monitoring all the profiles. Everything had to be read and approved before it was posted. I felt secure and began my search for a Christian woman I could talk to and possibly date.

I wrote my profile statement, Donna took my picture, and I was ready to go. It was great coming home in the evening to emails. Lo and behold, at the bottom of the screen were pictures of 5 women in my area looking for the same thing I was. A click on each picture brought up their profile detailing likes and dislikes, habits, family, and Church attendance. All in all, it gave me something to look forward to and at last I was getting out of my recliner and starting to do something that might satisfy my loneliness.

CM promoted an approach for the shy, referred to as a wink. There was a second little window that said something noncommittal, but invited members to make a comment of interest to another member. It had been over 40 years since I'd been single and vied for a lady's attention. I was grateful for a way to start out with baby steps.

I'll never forget my first experience with Carolina Gal. We commented on one another's profile, but we readily agreed that being 1,800 miles apart wasn't the best circumstance for a date.

Next, I emailed with a Christian-Jewish lady from New Jersey who had a second home in Texas. She asked me how far I lived from Abilene and asked if we could meet in the middle.

I was getting rather interested in the third lady from south Texas who called herself Blondena, but she never got around to posting a profile picture. When I went to her emails, there was the standard silhouette used for all females instead of her photo, so she never felt real. Eventually I gave up and moved on.

I'll never forget the woman in Kansas City. After only a couple of emails, she wrote that she could not do this any longer because she was still mourning her deceased husband of 3 years. The way I looked at it, she'd basically died with him 3 years earlier and was choosing to remain dead. It's a shame she'd paid her 6-month membership fee, posted her pictures, and wrote her profile only to abandon ship and swim back to her deserted island to waste away lying on top of his grave. I simply couldn't believe it.

In all my CM experiences, I saw only one red flag and it was when a woman wrote, "I believe there is a place for everything, and everything needs to be in its place." If that line won't cause El Slob-O to turn tail and run, nothing will. Most men are slobs, and as much as we loved our mothers, we don't want another one at this age!

There was a Colorado lady with her own business who made a huge deal out of the fact that her dead husband's name was the same as mine. She assured me that it was a sign from God! Looking back I realize she was just lonely like me and everybody else, but her eagerness scared me off.

Weirdest of all was the night I kept hearing a little beeping sound coming from my monitor. At the corner of my screen a small window was blinking with an occasional beep that said, "Someone wants to talk to you online." My option buttons were *talk now*, *maybe later*, and *not interested*. Out of frustration and curiosity I clicked on *maybe later* like an idiot and within 10 minutes, the beeping was back. The window said, "You have a message." So I read it. It was a 34-year-old, South African girl on a visit to Alabama who was looking for an American husband *now!* I don't know the whole story but she said, "I will marry you and be a good wife to you. And I don't care about our age difference." That age difference was 34 years, and I did care. She asked me to please respond and say if I was interested. The window was blinking again so this time I clicked *NOT INTERESTED* and that was the end of that.

Christian Mingle Wasn't the Answer

We found that the people on CM were just ordinary people, not Super-Christians. Members are not sorted and classified according to their stage of Christian maturity, level of church commitment, or their spiritual passion. They do ask how often their members attend church, and that information is posted. I say that because Ron and I found nothing extraordinary or magical in CM. Many people who hear our story initially consider the website to be the answer rather than God. It is not!

You might like to know the strategy we used to get God motivated to work in our behalf. We've discussed it endlessly since we found one another and here's the simple answer: We don't know. I was at the peak of my faith and Christian growth when John died, so being passionate wasn't the answer. My devotion to Christ didn't increase. I didn't join a prayer group, hook up with a TV evangelist, make a big donation, change denominations, commit to a small group, or start the "read the Bible in one year" program. I had done nothing new, bigger, or better that merited finding a Godly man.

When John died, I first looked nearby for a man. On Sundays, I spoke to a quiet, single gentleman who sat in the back row at my church. He'd been there for years, and I didn't even know his name. He'd always just been a part of the fixtures. After months of conversations with him, I learned that not everyone who is single wants to move from that spot. Some people might be willing to consider making a change if you have months or years to invest and if you're willing to wait for something that might never materialize. That was what I preferred about dating online. Everyone was looking for something, even if it wasn't the same thing. But it did prove they had arrived at the point where they knew they wanted a change.

I joined the same day Johnye called from Anchorage and told me about seeing a CM commercial. I had a few pictures of myself on my computer. Kenna took my picture on my sixtieth birthday sitting in a swing laughing. I realized it wasn't an attractive look to have my head back, my mouth wide open, and my eyes shut, but I hoped it would attract a man who wanted to laugh as well. It was a long shot, but weren't they all? I had more flattering pictures, but I wanted to post the truest representation of who I was and the way I actually looked in everyday life rather than on a special occasion. I knew if I ever met a man, I didn't want him to be let down because I didn't look as nice in person as I had in my pictures. In fact, I'd prefer the opposite, where he would be pleasantly surprised that I looked a little nicer than my pictures. In my profile as well as with my pictures, I tried to be totally honest. No one likes false advertisement where more is promised than can be delivered.

When I filled in the information on my profile, I said I was a courier. The little jobs I enjoyed doing around the farm could honestly qualify me as a courier if that's what I wanted to call myself. I wanted to be seen as the ordinary, hardworking 60-year-old widow that I was. I had an unimpressive job that required no special skills or education, and I wanted to attract that same type of man. After 36 years in agriculture, I knew what it was to face hard financial times. For 17 years, we had been in debt because of 2 hailstorms. However, I had finally accumulated a small savings that was entirely my own, and it made me feel rich even though I wasn't. I was willing to bring all that I had to a new relationship, but I didn't want to attract a man who was looking for a meal ticket. I wanted an old-fashioned gentleman like my dad who naturally expected to take care of his wife. If I said I was a partner in our farm I might seem like an easy target for a guy who was in debt because of an addiction or mismanaged finances.

The CM profile asked members if they were widowed or divorced, and it only allowed me to check one answer so I went with widowed, then mentioned in my profile that I was attending a Divorce Care Bible Study so men would know I'd been widowed and divorced.

I did such an amazing job of filling out my profile, being intentional and cautious, and saying witty things about my picture, that Ron and 2 other men were the only ones who ever sent me a wink or a smile. I'm glad Ron thought I was so terrific because no one else did. Looking back, I realize it was a blessing to be approached by the right man instead of getting sidetracked with a bunch of window-shoppers and missing the boat...correction-missing *my dreamboat!*

First Impressions

The First Time Ever I saw Her Face...

March 31, 2011 is a day that will go down in R. O. Gillespie history. I remember it well. I'd been on CM for close to a month and noticed there were new photos of area women posted at the bottom of my homepage. That night, she caught my eye. I read her profile and studied the rest of her pictures. I had to send her a comment. It was easy. It came from my heart.

"You have a beautiful smile. We live close enough that we could meet and go out for dinner or a movie."

I liked all of her pictures and her humorous remarks. I returned to her home page to look at her pictures frequently. When I realized that CM posted the number of return visits that were made to a member's profile and photos, I began to worry that she might think I was a stalker. I copied her pictures and saved them to my computer so I could look at her smile all I wanted.

k called herself Uniquely Regular and, brother, she was exactly that. She said she was a widow and a courier. I thought the picture of her holding the puppy in front of a Christmas tree was her small apartment. I'd seen small economy cars around town delivering for the pharmacies. I felt drawn to this poor, little girl who obviously needed someone to care for her and maybe take her out for a nice, nutritious meal.

In one photo, she was sitting on a rope swing with her head back, laughing. The thought of laughing with that happy lady clamped onto my heart. She made silly, witty comments to go with all of her pictures, and I thought they were wonderful. Here was a lady in a hard place who was enjoying her life in spite of everything.

She didn't use a picture of herself when she was younger or thinner. She didn't get out her glamor shots (though I've learned that she does have them). She just looked like a regular, everyday person that I could meet in a checkout line that might smile and strike up a conversation with a stranger just to be friendly. That friendly, average person was who I wanted to get to know, take out for coffee, and maybe invite to church.

He Loves Me, He Loves Me Not

I was picking up a load of wheat seed from Missouri for the farm. It was April 1, 2011, April Fools' Day. I had been on CM less than a week when I got Ron's first email. I had a brand new cell phone that got my emails, but I didn't know how to view his pictures or get to his profile information. I didn't want to commit sight-unseen to his invitation. I suggested a short coffee date just in case we didn't hit it off.

I was excited to get home and have a look at this boy. I remember looking into that sweet face and instinctively thinking, *He looks like someone who could love me.*

I had been rejected as a child, insecure as a wife, and devastated by my second marriage and divorce. My confidence was pretty much gone. Before John died, I wasn't wimpy. I was a strong, independent, take-charge type of woman. But that woman sunk in the quicksand around John's grave.

I didn't know how to enlarge Ron's profile pictures. In one of the photos he had on some sort of teeny-tiny, pink bowtie. I amazed myself because I was still willing to meet him even though I thought he might not be particularly masculine. I was mistaken about the pink bowtie. It was a red Nebraska Husker's emblem on his shirt and hat. I was especially mistaken about his masculinity.

Ron has told me that my profile reference to Divorce Care indicated to him that *I was probably damaged goods,* but he wasn't put off by it. He was confident that he could help me. Even before I responded to his first email he had started praying, "Lord, I could love this lady if you'll just give me a chance."

Our First Date at 60 and 68

Face-to-Face 😊

After 2 weeks of emailing, we still hadn't met or even set a date for meeting because I'd been in Missouri on a family genealogy trip with Gloria and Heidi. I took my laptop, but there were no internet connections or free time. After several frustrating days, I suspected that our budding relationship was in trouble.

I had been told that an email written in all caps meant the writer was shouting and angry, but k hadn't heard that. When she used all capital letters she thought it showed emphasis. I worried that I was saying something wrong and that she was offended because so much of what she wrote to me was in all capitals. Driving home, I was really down in the dumps trying to figure out what happened and where I went wrong!

When I got home there was a nice email and everything seemed just fine. k told me if we were going to meet for coffee, I needed to be the one to decide on the time and place. She was holding my feet to the fire. I was relieved.

In the meantime, she'd sent me a funny cartoon of an awful-looking lady sitting at her computer, hair in rollers, cigarette hanging out of her mouth, and wearing bunny slippers with long bunny ears. She said it was a picture of her. So at the end of my coffee date invitation I said, "Please do me a favor and don't wear your bunny slippers!"

Later that same afternoon, I opened up my work email and in big, bold letters the beginning line of an email from k read,

"I CHANGED MY MIND;
I DON'T WANT TO MEET YOU FOR COFFEE!"

My heart sunk. I didn't know what happened but she had clearly lost all interest in meeting me. I scrolled down a little further, and the email continued, "Because there is no way that you can be as funny in person as you are in your emails." Suddenly I was back on cloud-9again.

Finally, the day came that I was going to talk to a real person, face to face! I was tired of existing on emails alone. That morning I got up early and groomed with extra care. I drove over early and got us a quiet, cozy corner with comfortable chairs. I sat there in anticipation of what was going to happen any minute.

While I waited, I wondered, *What if she has car trouble or what if she goes to the wrong place?* I'd been looking forward to this moment for so long that if something went wrong or she didn't show up I was going to be more than disappointed.

k was late, which made the agony worse. Since then I've come to realize that it's normal for k to be late. The name she used on Christian Mingle was Uniquely Regular which was not only true but it intrigued me. I remember struggling to remain calm. I looked up and behold – Uniquely Regular was standing there before my very eyes.

She was tall and sleek, dressed in black slacks and a zebra-print shirt. As she walked towards me she recognized me, and our eyes met. All of a sudden there was that beautiful smile that I had admired so many times on her profile page. We exchanged hellos, and I finally had my opportunity to talk, but I was practically speechless. I snapped to and told my brain, "Come on, let's just do this. After all, you're a salesman. Get to showing the goods." So we walked up to the bar, and I ordered our coffees.

Sitting with our coffee, we told one another about our lives and circumstances and how we got to this place. We jumped from one subject to another. I remember especially liking it when she would tell me about a circumstance in her life, and I would indicate that I understood exactly what she was talking about and she'd reply, "Thank you." I'd never had anyone thank me for agreeing with them before. She was unique alright.

Coffee lasted 3-and-a-half hours, but the time flew by. I wanted it to last forever. After all, I certainly didn't want to go home to an empty house for the rest of the weekend.

By 2 in the afternoon, we had so much coffee that we needed a comfort break. When k came back from the ladies' room, she asked me if I was hungry. Of course I said yes. We agreed on a restaurant. I still remember being disappointed when she walked over to get in her own car, but I understood that it's best if a woman has control to leave at any time, so, I followed her in my pickup.

Learning to Live Again 😊

k had noticed on my profile that I like Michael W. Smith, a contemporary Christian singer. When she saw his posters in the church where she attended Divorce Care Bible Study, she forwarded his concert information to me while I was in Missouri. Before our first meeting, I bought 2 tickets fully intending to invite her to go with me if our meeting went well.

As I paid the check and we stood to leave, nothing had been said about the concert up to that point. k surprised me when she asked if I did anything about the MWS concert.

My instant reply was, "Yes, I bought 2 tickets."

From this part in the romantic meeting, my story heads south and really gets lame. When she asked me why I bought 2 tickets, I should have responded, "Well, it was in hopes of taking you." My dating skills were dusty after 40 years. I thought it would be cute to joke around. I actually said, "Well, I'm taking this homeless guy who hangs out around my office."

I expected her to respond, "Oh, I wanted to go." And I planned to say, "Then you're going! That homeless guy just lost out. I'd much rather be with you." That was the plan. As we were walking out of the restaurant, I was still trying to make it happen. Realizing how lame it came out, I came up with an amazing line to salvage the situation.

I said, "Ha-ha! I'm just kidding. I'm really taking my little sister."

Then matters actually went from bad to worse.

k turned to me and said, "Well, I hope you and your little sister have a wonderful time at the concert tomorrow." And she got in her car and drove off. I was an idiot! I hated myself then, and after all this time, I still hate the way I handled it just as much as I did that day in the parking lot. k always tries to console me by saying it was good for me to play hard to get. Actually, I wasn't playing hard to get, I was bungling.

When I told Donna about it, she immediately said, "Ronald Owen, could you not see this woman researched that concert so you could get tickets and invite her to go with you? You get on that phone right now and invite her to go with you. You have to explain that you were only kidding about the homeless guy and your sister."

I tried, but k had her ringer off while she was in her Divorce Care Class. Her class was meeting early because the class met in the same church that was hosting the MWS concert. One of the people in her class worked in the Christian bookstore where the tickets were being sold and had offered to buy tickets for anyone

Christian Mingle Profile Pictures

k looked like a friendly person I'd like to get to know, take out for coffee, and maybe invite to church.

The thought of laughing with this happy lady clamped on to my heart!

I looked into this sweet face and immediately thought, *He looks like someone who could love me.*

Ron's Young Years

Gillespie family starting at left: Taylor, Gloria, Leticia, Ron, seated Mom, Debbie, and Dad.

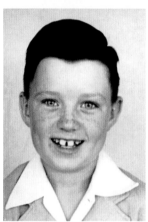

Miss Willie knighted me Sir Goose at our Tascosa High School pep rally.

I was so happy to leave the school band to play football.

Ron and Betty

When I was 13, Taylor and
I were close in size.

When I was 15, I could
have passed for his dad.

Eddie & Elberta Turner with me at their new house.

At the Grand Ole Opry
Betty laughed her head off.

Me & Betty

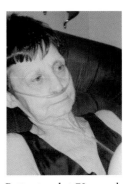

Betty stayed at 70 pounds
the last 3 years of her life.

k's Young Years

My harness looked like a dog leash.

My life was spent inside a picket fence.

I was 9 when Johnye was born.

144 pounds in the 6th grade

In 5th grade I was the tallest.

Until kindergarten I was a blonde.

By 1st grade my hair was brown.

I was a nerd in high school.

k and John

I was 30 and a "has been".

All I could think was, *What have I done?*

Jagee, Adam, and Justin.

John's pickup

Mel

10 weeks before the wreck. Beginning at top left the couples are John and me,
Becca & Adam, Jagee & Larry Dan. Bottom left is Steph holding Conner & Cole,
Justin hugging Jadan, the twins-Chaz & Kason, and Gage at right bottom corner.

Wedding and Travel

We married beneath the stars.

First Kiss

We could hardly wait.

Finally he had his arm around my shoulder.

Big Smiles &
Glowing Happiness

New York City

Alaskan Cruise

Ron's Bucket List - Scotland

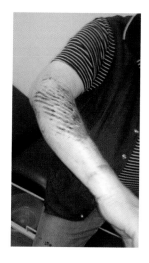

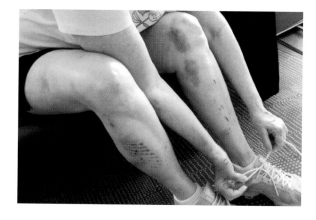

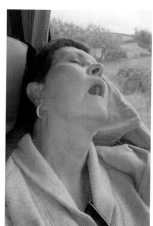

The pilots loved it when I said their cockpit looked
like the monitors in our farm combine back in Texas.
They put us in their seats and snapped our picture.

People in Our Story

Okly

Coffee Girls- Left Rochelle, top k, Courtney,
Doris, bottom row Debbie & Janice.

Mart and Minnie Crownover the
frisky/fun great-grandparents.

Acie Crownover
holding Husband.

Adam dancing with Acie

in the class at the discounted group rate. k made a point of telling me that there were no takers. I assumed she was telling me she didn't want to go. She said she was trying to tell me that she didn't have tickets already or a friend to go with.

That was our first miscommunication but not our last. The amazing thing about our relationship is the way we always manage to get things straightened out with a minimum amount of stress or hard feelings. Probably more than anything else, this makes our relationship fantastic. To this day we still haven't had an argument.

And just so you're not kept in suspense, I took my little sister to the MWS concert, and we did **NOT** have a wonderful time!

I Would Have If I Could Have

I was so anxious to meet Ron. I misunderstood where we were supposed to meet, and I was headed for the wrong place. I pulled into the parking lot at Hastings so I could put on lipstick before I drove down the street to meet Ron at Starbucks. I didn't want to take a chance that he'd be waiting in the parking lot and his first impression would be of me putting on my lip liner. I just happened to notice the name of the coffee shop in the bookstore was The Hardback Café, and that name seemed vaguely familiar, perhaps it was because this was the place we were supposed to be meeting! Oh my gosh! That was so typical of me. I thanked God and hurried inside.

I acted as if everything was fine instead of admitting my near miss. We talked forever. He was a very nice man. He seemed so sweet and genuine. As we talked about John and Betty, I knew I'd found a quality person in Ron.

But would there be any chance for us? I had no idea. I was

Ron's first date in over 40 years. He was as desperately lonely as I was. Unfortunately, being desperately lonely was enough to strike up a conversation, maybe even base a friendship on, but it absolutely was not enough for anything more. I wasn't in love, at least not yet. It was no secret that Ron was ready to find the right woman and get started moving in the right direction. I wanted that for both of us as well. I just wasn't sure if he was the one I wanted forever and always. I needed to FEEL SOMETHING MORE. I didn't know how to produce the feelings that weren't there. But I would have if I could have.

He Was Like a 5-Year-Old

I respected Ron for being a caregiver. My own dad had seen my mom through 4 brain tumor surgeries over a span of 15 years. After Mother died, I wish Dad could have found someone to love him those last 10 years while he was all alone.

I didn't realize it, but I projected all of the endearing feelings I had for my dad onto Ron. Perhaps that's the reason my strongest initial feelings for him were of respect and admiration. Ron openly approved of me, and he was anxious for me to feel what he was feeling. I wanted to feel what he was feeling, but it simply wasn't there. I remember thinking he was like a 5-year-old who was having his first crush on his kindergarten teacher. It was very flattering. This man had become dear and precious to me in our very first meeting and from that moment it has only grown stronger and sweeter. It took a long, long time before I actually fell deeply and passionately in love with Ron, 2 weeks to be exact. I'm confident on the time because 2 weeks after that first meeting, I proposed marriage to Ronald Owen Gillespie.

3 Strikes, But Not Out

As we were walking out of the restaurant, I asked Ron if he had plans for the rest of the day. I thought I'd like to stay in town and talk more with him, but he said that he had other plans. Not only did he make no effort to keep me in town to visit more, but he didn't mention seeing me ever again. He had shot me down 3 times in the few minutes it took to walk from the restaurant table to my car. On my drive home, I wondered if my kindergarten student had thrown his teacher under the bus for some cute little thing with pigtails. What if there was a woman on CM that he liked more than he liked me? From the looks of things, he might have eliminated me already. On my drive home, I thought hard to come up with a legitimate question that I could casually ask him that would require a reply. When I walked in my front door, I walked straight to my computer. I had to make certain that he hadn't forgotten me already. I wanted him to stay on the hook until I determined if he was the one!

A Moment to Realize

Ron's good memory of our meeting is overshadowed by his remorse over the concert bungle. He never believes me when I tell him things worked out for the best, and I honestly believe they did. The reason I didn't get tickets was because I didn't want to go to the concert alone and then drive back to Dumas, alone, after dark. Though it was clear that he approved of me at our meeting, when he didn't offer me his other ticket it told me he wasn't to be had easily. It gave me a moment to realize that I really did want to hear from him again.

I turned on my cell phone as soon as my Divorce Care Class

ended. Ron called to invite me but our reception was awful and he kept cutting in and out, but I got the general idea of what he was saying. He doesn't realize that I got what I wanted–he invited me! The concert was so unimportant. I couldn't have cared less about going. I just wanted to make certain that Mr. Gillespie wanted to see me again!

Hey Look at Me - I'm Dating!

Almost Kicked to the Curb

The first time I went to k's house we walked her dog, and she'd made a comment about a potential suitor she'd kicked to the curb because he was such a big fan of a certain political talk show host. At one time, I'd been somewhat of an interested listener to that dude myself. If she chopped some guy's head off for listening to a talk show, how secure was I? It made me feel as if I was walking through a mine field. One wrong move and it would all be over. That night when I got home from Dumas, she had sent me an email. She said I seemed so uncomfortable talking to her, and she compared it to hand-to-hand combat. She suggested we find a project we could work on instead of sitting in the living room while we talked. It felt as if we were sliding backwards, and I didn't know how to stop it. I woke at 4 a.m. and couldn't go back to sleep. After a couple of hours of praying and thinking, I felt the Holy Spirit come over me and realized what I needed to do was relax and be myself, no fears, and no pretense. And then if it didn't work out, it just wasn't meant to be. I got up and on the road because this breakthrough had to be delivered face to face.

When I arrived, it was still early so I called to see if she was up and ready for a visit. She immediately asked me if I'd already read the email she'd just sent me. I was afraid that she'd sent me a *Dear John letter* before she even heard me out. I was too late! I explained that I hadn't read her email because I wasn't at home, I was in Dumas.

There was more misunderstanding and confusion as I waited

for her to come join me for coffee, and she waited for me to arrive at her house. As the minutes ticked by, we were both becoming more anxious. Finally, I called her and we got the plan straight.

When I got to her house, she left her grandsons inside watching TV, and she came out to the driveway and sat with me in my pickup. If she didn't even invite me into her house that was a sure sign that she was giving me the ax.

When she climbed up in my truck, I said, "k, I wasn't myself the other night. The Holy Spirit told me if I would just be honest and relax then everything would be alright." I felt there was little to lose at this point, so I boldly told her everything right up front. "God is my source, and I've been praying for him to lead me to a good Christian woman. And k, I believe you're the one."

Then I looked her in the eye and reached across the console and for the very first time ever I touched her as I took hold of her hand. Her expression was hard to read. Later when I got back home and read her email, her expression made a little more sense. She had written me that we ought to start out as friends, and that meant no physical contact including holding hands.

So I'd just broken rule number one. This wasn't going to be easy.

Trying not to Scare Him Off

From the beginning, I saw Ron as a priestly sort of guy. I suppose it was because he was open about his spiritual convictions and frequently referred to God as his source. I was accustomed to the way the Christian men in my life got a deer-in-the-headlights look if the uncomfortable subjects of God, faith, or prayer came up. In contrast, Ron seemed spiritual and holy. I tried to hold back just a tad on my smart-alecky wise cracks. I wanted to bring Ron along slowly so I wouldn't scare him off before he could get adjusted to my constant humor.

Lose that Pucker, Mister!

The day after Ron and I met, he went to the Michael W. Smith Concert without me. That same day, my Divorce Care Bible Study topic was intimacy. The lesson encouraged singles not to confuse physical intimacy with genuine intimacy. The study book said when dating turns sexual, the focus of the relationship is no longer to get to know one another better. I didn't want our focus to turn from relational to sexual. I was in the market for a man who was absolutely certain that he wanted k Crownover! I knew I had a quirky sense of humor, a different personality, and plenty of other goofy qualities that not everyone could appreciate. I liked to laugh and have fun and I never shut it off. I wanted this new man to get a good look at the comedian in me and think long and hard about whether he wanted to live with a clown. Furthermore, I was not going to audition for the role as the wife. If I suited Ronald, he could make up his mind without free samples!

I was a little nervous about taking such a bold stand against physical contact. I didn't know if that would be the last straw. My extreme position might run this guy off, but I truly felt God had intentionally timed that week's Bible study to be about intimacy. *After all, why was I reading the Bible and praying for guidance if I didn't believe that God was interested in my life and that all I was studying at that same time was God's way of leading me.* I got up early that morning and carefully worded a firm but friendly explanation of my new, but non-negotiable policy concerning the direction of our relationship - if there was to be a relationship after he read what I had to say.

I emailed Ron, "If we were going to start our relationship based on friendship, then we ought to behave as friends. I don't hold hands, kiss, or allow my friends to sit with their arm around my shoulder. So that's what I propose for the duration of our friendship. I don't want sex to distract us from the onset and get us sidetracked from building a quality relationship. First things first, and the first thing needs to be a friendship."

I had just sent Ron that email when he called me. I asked him if he'd read it because he needed to before we talked. He said he couldn't because he was already in Dumas. As I waited for him to arrive at my house, I became more and more nervous. Finally he called, and we'd miscommunicated. He was waiting for me while I was waiting at home for him. I didn't want to hear what he might have to say because I felt it would probably all go down the drain after he read my "new policy notification" email. I wanted us to have a private conversation, so I left my grandsons in the house and went out to join Ron. Sitting in my driveway, I could hardly pay attention to what Ron was saying about God being his source and believing that I was the woman he'd been praying for. He was so sweet and courageous to say those wonderful things and reach across the console and take hold of my hand, but I couldn't enjoy the moment for worrying. I would seem cold and indifferent if I didn't allow him to take my hand while he poured his heart out. But if I did hold his hand then when he read my email about no physical contact it might appear I'd changed my mind. The only way to prevent sending mixed signals would be to stop his speech and explain my email. But I'd worked a long time to find the exact wording for my email, and I wasn't going to toss it out the window and blurt out everything to him haphazardly. Plus, I wanted him to read it while he was alone and take the time to really think about whether he could go along with my decision.

To you this may not seem like such a big deal since our courtship was so brief, but the day I delivered my ultimatum I had no idea if we might be dating for months or even years. I think you'll agree that for most men that would have been the end.

She Was A Little Extreme

When I left k's driveway that morning and got home to read her email, I was shocked. I'd never heard of such a thing. It struck me as overkill. I was positive I could hold k's hand, put my arm around her shoulder, and even kiss her without letting things get out of control. But if that was what she really thought we ought to do, I was willing to go along.

Could Passion Fit Through a Key Hole?

I didn't have those passionate feelings that were so important for me to feel before I could move into something deeper than respect and friendship. I felt the same respect for Ron that I felt for my father, but I certainly didn't want to be married to my father. But how could those sexual feelings come if I had the doors locked and bolted to physical touch? If that question had occurred to me, I might have worried about it, but it didn't. I was just obeying God, being myself, and having tons of fun with a very nice man who seemed to never tire of my personality. I was in heaven!

Flirting Made Easy

I quickly recruited Ron to texting. Most seniors aren't interested in texting, but it was perfect for me when I was helping out at the farm. I frequently had long waits in a remote field without any cell phone service. Even though I couldn't make a call, I could compose text messages. I'd turn off my pickup, roll down the window, pull out my phone, and start texting. Then later, when I got closer to town and had service, I would send my messages.

You're Kidding, THIS is Love?

My big fingers made it hard to text on the little cell phone keyboard, but if that was k's game, then I would find a way to do it! I was at work when my nephew, Russ, heard the constant text notifications as her messages kept pouring in. He came out of his office to see what all the racket was about. Russ got a big kick out of me struggling to learn how to text.

He laughed and said, "Uncle Ron, I think that chick really loves you."

I had barely taken that thought in when Cari said, "Don't listen to Russ, he doesn't know what he's talking about!"

This new style of dating and communicating was confusing. Could these text messages really be love? Wow, things had certainly changed since I dated back in high school!

Seriously Looking For FUN

If I had a choice between being drop dead gorgeous, fabulously wealthy, and never growing old, or always having fun and being happy, I would choose fun and happy.

The first time I saw what it was to have fun and be happily married came the day after I married John. We went to the Crownover family reunion, and I was introduced to his extended family. I remember sitting at the table with his grandmother and all the married ladies. As Grandpa walked past us, Minnie held out her tea glass and asked if he'd refill it. He smiled and asked her what she'd give him in return for the favor.

She asked him, "What do you want?"

He answered, "What do you have?"

Much to my amazement, a grandmother wearing a hairnet said, "I've got anything you want!"

With a huge smile Mart snatched up her glass and trotted off to get her refill as happy as if he were going to take her up on their bargain as soon as he returned!

That was my first time to see frisky interaction between a man and his wife. Even in the movies, flirting was never between a married couple, and John's grandparents were actually being sexually playful right in front of their daughters and granddaughters! How I loved it! Mart and Minnie made it look like so much fun. They weren't putting on a show, it was their normal behavior. Looking back, I see that God was showing me how enjoyable and fun life and marriage could be. I wanted to be like them. Since John and I were just getting started, and we had nothing hurtful between us to drag us down, it looked as if we could have taken that inspiration and ran with it. It was perfect timing for us to get a head start toward marital bliss, but we hardly ever flirted, and we didn't understand that having fun had more to do with attitude than activity. We were just young.

After John died, it seemed that I'd missed the boat on playful flirting. But when I married as a senior citizen, I realized that all was not lost. Ron and I flirt. We are fun. We hope we'll be as inspirational as Mart and Minnie were. We're careful to be genuine and not put on a show. We're excited about what God has brought to us and what He has done inside of us. Sometimes our joy is contagious and sometimes it's not. Many of our family and friends give us a patronizing smile, pat us on the head, and assure us we're still in our honeymoon phase but eventually we'll settle down and become a normal married couple just like them. We pray to God that they are wrong!

What I Could Have Died for

I was driving the 45 miles of nice, divided 4-lane highway on my way home from k's at about 10:30 one night. I hadn't gone far when I received a text message, and I knew it had to be from her. I glanced down for just one second and read, "How long do you think before we're ready to move to the next level?" It took me by surprise, but it wasn't nearly as shocking as when I looked up again and realized where I was. The highway had veered to the left and directly ahead was the entrance to a roadside park. I was entering that roadside park at 70-miles-per-hour with 18-wheelers lining both sides of the narrow rest area.

This is the type of thing you would expect to see in a movie like *Smoky and the Bandit* with special effects or a stunt driver, but there were no special effects or stunt drivers, just me. I remember trying to stop my pickup and praying, "Oh God, please don't let any of these truck doors come open because there's not enough room." At a normal 20-miles-per-hour it wouldn't have been a problem to stop for an opening door, but at 70 and it being pitch dark out, it was a horrifying thought. When I was able to get the truck stopped without incident, and I regained my composure, I looked in my rearview mirror and saw lights popping on in every truck cab. I felt it was time to ease out of the park and back onto the highway. I didn't want the truckers I woke up coming after me.

I learned the next day that k's idea of "moving to the next level" only meant going steady! I almost died for that?

A Giddy High

I knew there were many more females looking for males than men looking for women. I thought it would be smart to hog tie and put my brand on my new little buddy before someone better than me scooped him up. I wanted to think of a way to ask Ron to be exclusive without sounding pitiful or pushy, so I pulled out my favorite tool and used my humor. I thought he'd think it was cute if I used a throwback term like going steady. He thought it was a fun idea, and we teased back and forth about it. I said I needed either his I.D. bracelet or his St. Christopher necklace to seal the deal. I suggested that at our age it would be tacky unless his name was written in diamonds. He didn't bite.

The first Valentine's Day after we married, Ron gave me a St. Christopher pendant with little diamonds around the edge. I love the way he remembers my jokes and turns them into gifts or cards. He does little things that show he's thinking about me all the time. I'm flattered every time he comes up with a new password, and he makes it about me. My favorite is Ronlk4evr (Ron loves k forever). He's so clever. I think he ought to write a book!

The idea of flirting and being silly is a hard concept to sell to serious people who are bogged down with aches and pains. It's unfortunate because laughter brings relief. It had been more than 40 years since Ron or I had felt the giddy high that romance and flirting brings. We can testify that there is something about it that sparks energy and enthusiasm even at our age.

Alligator for Breakfast

By the time he rolled out of bed each morning, I usually had an email or a text message waiting for him. I knew I should be more ladylike and exhibit some restraint, but I couldn't hold myself back.

After sending "I hope you have a great day" 2 mornings in a row, I felt dull and unimaginative. I decided to be cute and say something with a little pizazz. I used his morning water aerobics class as my inspiration and texted, "Hey Tarzan, Jane's hungry, so get out of that muddy river and go wrestle up an alligator for breakfast."

To which he immediately replied, "Tarzan want to please woman," and suddenly, 5 silly little words produced the feelings I needed before I could be more than just a friend to Ronald Gillespie. Even now, they still make me smile and blush a little because that was the first time I felt, well, you know...

Ron had "JANE" engraved inside my wedding band, and I had "TARZAN" engraved in his. Without holding my hand, putting his arm around my shoulder, or even kissing my forehead, I was getting *the hots* for some 68-year-old priestly guy. God can obviously do a lot with a little.

Bag Lady Without a Stick

If I'd drawn a line down a page and listed the pros and cons about Ron on either side, the con side would have been empty. Ron was an amazing Christian man, easy going, happy, and best of all, he liked my sense of humor. Since the Tarzan thing, I was starting to get a little turned on. Still, I had to be sure.

Are you dying to know how I fell in love with Ron? After church, on Easter Sunday, I had dinner at Ron's house and met the majority of his family. As he showed me through his house, he mentioned that he recently ordered new furniture for the master bedroom. The next day I texted him about his new furniture as I drove to Dodge City, Kansas, in an old farm pickup. The road was under repair with orange cones and deep drop offs on both sides, not good conditions for texting even if I'd been the passenger, but I didn't let that stop me from driving and texting. (Don't try it.)

I intended to compose a message that conveyed the thought, "You might want to wait on buying new furniture. The woman you marry will probably have a house full of furniture. You may like her bedroom furniture and want to keep it. And even if she doesn't have a single stick of furniture, I bet she'd want to help you select your new bedroom furniture."

That was the plan.

As usual I was trying to be witty, driving dangerously, and fighting with a brand new cell phone that offered predictive text suggestions. I don't remember exactly how I worded my long message, but I do remember the last part of the message. I meant to text, "...even if you fall in love with a bag lady without a single stick of furniture – she'd still enjoy helping you select new furniture..." I noticed I didn't get the "t" in "stick" so the word in my message was "sick". I tried to replace it with one of the predictive text suggestions. There were several choices. One of the first suggested words was *suck*, next was *stick*, another suggested word was *dick*. Don't forget that I'm driving on a 2-lane road that's being repaired. I intended to tap "stick" but somehow I touched both the other suggested words instead. I don't know how it happened! I couldn't believe it! I panicked! The send button on my new phone was in the same place where the delete button had been on my old cell phone. I bet you can guess what happened next...

Yes, you read it right! I had sent my boyfriend, the priestly guy, the 2 nastiest words I'd seen written inside a convenience store's bathroom stall. I was so horrified that I almost drove off the road! Even so, there was no way to retract an erroneous text message.

It was time for Ron to be getting out of water aerobics. I normally had a flirty greeting waiting for him, and he always responded immediately. As soon as I sent that vile message, I found a place to pull off the highway, and I started apologizing in earnest. I was sending one text message right after the other begging for forgiveness and explaining as fast as I could. But evidently Ron was really offended because he wasn't answering, and his silence was killing me.

I later learned that Ron stayed late that morning to rent a day locker after his class. When he got in his pickup and turned on his phone, all my messages started rolling in. He said he felt sorry for me, and he wanted to do more than just say it was okay and that he understood.

He replied, "Hey, tell your son if the farm ever goes broke, not to worry because his mom can make a fortune with a 'dirty text line' message service!" He hoped that would set my mind at ease and help me feel better. But he did much more. He became the man I was looking for. I had found someone who could release the tension of an embarrassing situation. My life was full of goof ups, and I had always wanted a man who could laugh it off and go on. The Minnie Crownover in me had found her Mart! I was so in love!!!!!

The Clowns Took over the Circus

Ron has a great sense of humor, and he never gets tired of mine. Betty and John were the serious type. They say opposites attract and obviously they do, because 2 serious people married 2 people who loved to joke and tease. Betty and John permitted our antics and sometimes they would join in the laughter. Other times they would give the "enough is enough" look that signaled it was time to stop the wise cracks and settle down. Ron married Betty and I married John knowing full well they weren't clowns. Betty and John did a good job of keeping a tight lid on the daily humor. Being mature and serious is good, but being fun is just as good. Since Ron and I married, I guess you could say the clowns have taken over the circus, and we're running the show. We think it's funny to tell our stories about falling down on the escalator, running out of gas on my birthday, and getting lost in downtown Paris in the middle of the night. We go to sleep and we wake up talking and laughing and in a good mood. Though Ron and I get upset with others, we've never been upset with one another and we hope that never changes!

Marriage Proposals

You Wanna Get hitched?

I proposed to Ron at Pescaraz restaurant after 2 long weeks of dating. We were talking excitedly, and it seemed everything we said was preceded by "if" – if we get married, if this leads somewhere, if we have a future together, and if this works out. Finally, I'd had enough of the ridiculous "ifs" and without any forethought, I blurted out, "If you'd just decided whether you want to marry me or not, we could cut this conversation in half." He looked as if I'd thrown cold water on him. I was a little shocked myself. I hadn't planned on proposing that night or ever. I had the bad habit of putting my mouth in drive and giving it the gas before I turned my brain on.

Sticking with My Original Plan

All along I'd planned to propose to k at my house on Saturday. I could have proposed the night before at Pescaraz, but I didn't want to propose in a public place. I had prepared what I was going to say. I was a little nervous. Even though I'd been married twice before, I'd never proposed. I wanted this to be something special for both of us to remember. I was glad that at least I didn't have to be worried about her answer. As I was rehearsing my proposal and she was driving over to my house, she called to suggest a wedding date that was only 2 weeks away. With all that, I felt pretty confident she was going to say *yes*.

Even with it settled that she would marry me; I still wanted to give her a proposal that would be memorable. When she arrived, I took her to the living room, sat her down on my couch, knelt down on one knee, took her by the hand, and asked her to marry me. Lo and behold, she said *yes*.

2 + 2 + 2 = Not 2 Long

With our wedding only 2 weeks away, I asked Ronald what he wanted to do about kissing. I was certainly ready for our first kiss if he was. Without hesitation, he said he'd come to believe it honored me and it honored God for us to wait. Ron liked the idea of completely abstaining from everything physical, even our first kiss, until the preacher said, "You may kiss your bride." So for the rest of our engagement, we remained kiss-less. I was impressed with his desire to honor God and me by waiting. Every single thing he said and did just made me love and respect him more.

I'm so happy that we waited on that first kiss because Ron doesn't just give a little peck of a kiss. I'd seen kisses like his in the movies, but I'd never had one. His kisses are the start of something big rather than a casual way to say farewell and goodnight.

Our timeline is easy to explain; we emailed for 2 weeks, dated for 2 weeks, and were engaged for 2 weeks. It was 6 weeks from my first email reply until our wedding! While we were emailing and dating we had no clue that our relationship was traveling in the express lane.

Getting off on the Right Foot

In one weekend, Ron and I made our 3 most important decisions. First, we agreed to marry. Second, we set the wedding date. Third, we decided where we would live. You can't appreciate the significance of the decision about where we would live unless you know about my past.

Not ANOTHER Childhood!

John was so nice and easy to get along with that in the short amount of time we dated, we never had an argument. I was head over heels in love with him and eager to be a good wife. Growing up, neither of us had many friends, but after the wedding we finally had a real friend in each other. He was truly a sweetheart, and I adored him. I couldn't help asking him all sorts of silly questions because I wanted to know him inside and out. All his likes and dislikes mattered to me because I wanted to please him, and I knew he wanted to please me just as much.

After our first month of marriage, John moved our trailer from town to the farm and parked us in his parent's yard with our front door facing theirs. I hadn't made any friends in Dumas, so I liked the idea of being around his family. But once we got to the farm, things changed. No longer did we get up, eat a fast breakfast, and rush around to get him off to work. Instead John got dressed, he skipped eating breakfast with me, and he drove his pickup a few hundred feet from our front door to theirs. He left his pickup idling while he went inside, and he seemed to stay for a long time at his parents' while I stood at my window and watched. He never asked me to go with him. His folks never invited me over, and I was too busy fuming and pouting to think of walking over uninvited just to see what the big attraction was. Being on the outside looking in, it felt as if I was repeating my childhood. My zeal faded as I realized that I would never fit in at the farm as I had hoped.

John said we couldn't afford the gas for me to drive the 60 miles to see my parents, but he left his pickup idling every single morning while he went inside to visit with his.

When I confronted him about it, he merely said, "Stopping and starting is hard on an engine, and it needs to warm up."

I was especially irked that we couldn't afford gas, but he could afford to smoke. This was the original tear in our relationship. I was isolated while he saw his family every day. I couldn't even call my parents because we didn't have a phone for the 4 years we lived on the farm.

I saw that John had simply added me to his life without giving up anything. He still lived in the country, saw his folks daily, and kept his pickup and car so he didn't have to get my permission for anything. I gave up living in the city, seeing my family, and having the freedom to do as I pleased, just so I could be his wife. Worst of all, John didn't appreciate my sacrifice for the sake of our marriage regardless of how much I complained about it. Why did I have to give up everything while he gave up absolutely nothing? Marriage just wasn't fair! Keep in mind that even though I was a wife, I was still a teenager. I came to realize that maybe he wasn't as eager to please me as I had been to please him...in the beginning.

I Learn the Hard Way

I met my second husband through a dating service called *It's*

Just Lunch. I told him the night we met that I hoped to get married and for my second marriage to be even better than my first. He was shocked by my straightforwardness. Long story short, he insisted we date more than a year, so we did. I broke up with him many times during our 15-month courtship. He didn't want to marry me, but he didn't want me to get away. Finally, I broke it off for the last time and sent him away for good. It was at that point he surrendered and agreed to marry me rather than let me get on with my life. I thought I was smarter than his 2 previous wives, and where they had failed I would succeed. He would be happy being married to me. After all, it stood to reason that he would try his hardest to make our marriage work because what man would want 3 divorces? That's what I thought, and I was wrong. He'd already had 2 wives pack up their half and leave him. He was better prepared to protect himself against wife number 3 and a possible third divorce.

We didn't make any definite plans for our future, not even which of our houses we would live in. Instead, we got married with a "wait and see where this goes" attitude. It worked great! We definitely saw where it went. Halfway through our wedding night, he lost all interest in me, and he never got any of it back. Our marriage was completely over in less than 4 hours. After the wedding, he never came to Dumas and spent the night with me again.

When I wanted to go be with him in Amarillo, he told me, "No, it's inconvenient."

I asked him, "Then why did you marry me?"

He said, "I thought I loved you."

When I asked him what was wrong, he answered, "I'm more independent than I realized."

Finally, I gave up when he told me there was nothing I could do to make our marriage work.

I didn't want to get a divorce and be a failure. I actually postponed the court date until our second anniversary so it wouldn't "sound so bad". I was humiliated beyond words. Admittedly, I learned a lot from my second marriage and divorce, and I learned all of it the hard way.

I didn't want to be Jell-O

I hoped Ron would want to live in my house because Stephanie had moved all of John's clothes to the garage closet soon after he died, and over the next few months, I gave them away. But Betty had been dead for 2 years and all of her things were still exactly where she left them in her bathroom, dresser, and closets. I thought if I moved into their house, I would be allotted "her old space." I would feel like liquid Jell-O that must conform to the shape of a mold.

I told Ron that I wished we'd sell both of our houses and get a new one. I explained that I would always be asking him, "Where did you and Betty put this or that?" What I meant was, "If I move into the house that belonged to you and Betty, I'll always feel as if I'm an outsider only here to fill in temporarily." Ron just thought I was worried about learning my way around the kitchen. He assured me that he'd help me find things, and he assumed that eased my concerns. The main thing he wanted was to get his house paid off before he traded for a different house.

I drove home that night dejected and feeling that Betty and John had been our real mates. I was stupid to think our marriage could be anything compared to the marriages we had lost. Ron had done a good job of laughing off my mistakes about the bag lady and Tarzan, but up to that point, all our words were *only words*. I had been assuming that we were madly in love, but it was time for a reality check. Ours wasn't a storybook romance, and I wasn't a princess that Ron was coming to rescue. By the time I reached Dumas, I was down in the dumps and ready to toss my dreams out the car window. Truth was - Ron and I were nothing but creaky old senior citizens.

It was scary to think that it was the first day of the rest of our lives. I thought about how impossible it was to drive straight on a dirt road if ruts had been made after a rain. Those deep muddy tracks were practically magnetic the way they seemed to tug at my tires. The moment one tire fell into a rut, the rest of my tires fell into their ruts and suddenly steering was impossible.

That night I realized Ron and I were about to make some deep ruts in our relationship. The way I handled this first, major disappointment would matter. Ron hadn't understood how important the new house was to me, and he didn't get the seriousness of the situation, but I did. The question was, "How would I handle it this time?" When I was married before, I'd tried everything from pouting to standing my ground, but nothing had ever worked. I couldn't think of what to do so I decided to try something I had never done before. I took a deep breath, got a good attitude, and decided to cooperate with Ron's decision about the house. If he wanted to marry me, I wasn't going to waste my last chance at a good life by demanding my own way. I didn't want God to regret giving me what I'd been praying for. So, I just got happy even though I didn't get my way!

When I saw Ron the next day, the first thing he said was, "I thought about what you said last night and it made sense. It would be best if we sold our houses, bought a new home, and got a fresh start for both of us."

I felt as if a curse had been broken. The next day our realtor showed us 3 houses, all on the same block, and we had the third house bought before our wedding. I didn't mess around.

Starting out equal and both of us sacrificing 100% was perfect. We gave up our larger homes and downsized into a smaller house. It was a true fresh start. It proved that I was more than a fill-in for Betty, and that this wasn't an extension of either of our old marriages.

I learned that Ron's sweet words weren't empty and neither were mine.

I love that Ron thinks my opinion is important. I'm amazed when he decides to go with my recommendations. When we were dating he often said, "You're worth it," but that was only a nice sentiment until he proved it by respecting me and my opinion. I don't have to pout or stand my ground because Ron is good enough to hear me out, and that alone is satisfying.

Overcoming Obstacles, Barriers, & Objections

Missing Family Support 😊

I can't give my family enough credit for the way they helped fill the emptiness after Betty died. My entire social network was my family. Whether I was going to dinner, plays, concerts, or just walking, I could take Donna. We filled a void for one another at the end of each work day. Since Taylor had died several years earlier, I was already somewhat of a father figure to my niece, Kristie, her husband, and twin sons. Once Betty was gone, it helped me to have Kristie's family take up some of my spare time. I was in constant communication with Donna and Kristie, calling and emailing several times each day. But by the time Betty had been gone 2 years, I felt guilty that I was probably overusing both of these relationships.

Once I started dating k, she became my entire world. My relationships with Donna and Kristie took a nosedive, and I immediately became the guy who had deserted his family. I had felt so guilty for needing my family to get me through my loneliness that I completely forgot I was also filling a void in their lives. I expected them to be relieved when I married and left them to return to life as usual. I was wrong, but I didn't see it at the time. I just wanted them to be as happy for me as the rest of my family was.

When I told Leticia and Gloria about my engagement, they both communicated confidence that I was old enough, as well as spiritually and emotionally mature and healthy enough, to know my own mind and make my own decision. They didn't encourage me to wait. They had nothing negative to say. They had only one thing in their hearts and that was for me to be happy with the woman I loved for the rest of my life.

But Donna and Deb advised me to wait a few more months. When they told me their objections, I was amazed at their logic. One reason we needed to wait was because I'd never had a fight with k or even seen her mad. I thought that was a good thing, but evidently they didn't. Then they felt it was unfair that k had met all of the Gillespies at my house on Easter Sunday, but they hadn't met her family yet. That was really nuts because they had never met any of Betty's family in 39 years and neither had I. If anyone should have been interested in meeting k's family it should have been me, but I wasn't. In fact, I didn't meet them until they arrived for our wedding.

k made me feel better when she said it proved to her that I was completely committed since I wouldn't allow my family to dissuade me. She's right; it would have been easy for me to allow my sisters' arguments to discourage me since I'd relied so heavily on them for the past 7 years. But when you know something is right for you, you can't wait until every significant friend and family member gives their approval, or you'll never make a move. I wish all my sisters had been thrilled. They could have said k would make a perfect wife for me since we got along so well. It just didn't happen that way. I knew if there was a choice to be made, I would choose a future as a married man over remaining single and depending solely upon my family to fill my days for the rest of my life.

Blackballed?!

Believe it or not, when Ron's younger sisters wanted him to hold off on marrying me, I wasn't hurt. I assumed they thought I was a gold-digger and that amused me. It didn't even bother me that Ron's pastor told him he had only 2 words for him concerning me, and they were *slow and SLOWER!* That rolled off my back. We hadn't been married very long when we learned that Jay was asked to talk Ron out of marrying me or at least to refuse to perform the ceremony. That came as a big surprise, but it wasn't hurtful since it wasn't successful.

Why would anyone think it would be a good idea for us to put off marriage? Ron and I weren't getting any younger, healthier, prettier, richer, or smarter. We're senior citizens, not seniors in high school. In high school, everyone was on the lookout for a date and a mate, but finding a fit at our age was no small thing. Ron and I know a widowed man and a widowed lady who allowed their adult children to shame them out of dating. That was 15 years ago. Since then, neither of them ever met a second person that they were interested in dating. Now the widow's children use her for a babysitter. The widower's children are ready for him to find a nice lady because they are tired of him hanging around on Sundays. And the only crimes these 2 people committed were to survive the death of their spouse and to allow their family to undermine their decisions.

I'm so delighted that Ron had prayed for *a nice Christian lady*. God couldn't have dropped one in his lap any plainer if He had flown a helicopter over Ron's backyard and parachuted a lady carrying a Bible down to him.

The way I look at it, family support is overrated. Ultimately, each member of the Gillespies will decide for themselves whether to give me the thumbs up or the thumbs down, the same as they decided about Betty.

Ron and I have had several heart-to-heart talks with family members. Some understood. Some have refused to understand. With some the jury is still out, but it doesn't matter because we are happy regardless! We're glad that we didn't let anyone stop us.

What's Inheritance Got to Do with It?

After John died, I was so unhappy. It was obvious that I wouldn't remain single if I could help it. Before I started dating, my sons asked me to be mindful of the farm. They were right. A divorce could put the farm at risk. Our farm was not only where the 5 of us were employed, it was our family's legacy. From the beginning, I knew I would get a prenuptial agreement if I ever married again. It was a sound business precaution.

The prenuptial made it easier for my children to accept my marriage to a man they had never met. It was a simple way to prove that neither Ron nor I had anything to hide or ulterior motives. After John's death, I had promised my sons their fair share of the farm because of their lifetime involvement, and the prenuptial agreement prevented the need for concern and awkward questions.

I would much rather scrub toilets than talk to accountants and attorneys, but I forced myself to get their help because I wanted good financial planning for the future. I appreciated how very generous my children had been with me since they took over the farm after John's death. I'm especially pleased with the way they accepted Ron into our family without hesitation even before they knew him very well.

The Village Idiot

I lived in a small town of about 13,000. All 3 of my children had outstanding accomplishments and even the people who had never met me knew who Justin, Jagee, and Adam were and that k Crownover was their mom. After my short marriage to my second husband, I felt that I was the village idiot, and my personal life was breaking news in every coffee shop in Dumas. The way I finally set myself free from my fears was to accept that there's not much new to talk about in a small town. And I would hate to see some other widow miss an opportunity to marry and be happy because she was afraid of what I might say about her to my coffee friends. It finally boiled down to whether I would settle for being the village idiot or the *lonely* village idiot because the past was unchangeable but my future was hanging in the balance. That's the way I overcame my fears about gossip in a small town and was able to get on with my life.

Mirror, Mirror, on the Wall... It's Only Me

I never considered myself a pretty girl or a beautiful woman, but the first time a young cashier took one look at me and decided I qualified for a senior discount, I was insulted! It was one thing not to feel particularly attractive, but it was entirely different to know I looked old. That made it especially hard to imagine dating again. All I could see were all the things that were wrong or weird about me. For one thing, my perfect, youthful plumbing had slipped, and there had been a terrifying incident where either a valve didn't close completely or maybe it was my gasket that didn't seal securely but regardless there was a teensy-tiny microscopic problem with a little bit of seepage. In my moment of private humiliation, I would have gladly flagged down the Death Angel if he'd been passing by, but he wasn't around to help me out in my hour of need. Though this was a once in a lifetime, isolated case, I have been a nervous wreck dreading that it might someday happen a second time. It took a lot of courage to invite a new husband into my personal space. I'm glad I didn't get scared and chicken out!

I Am What I Am, and That's All That I Am

My appendix ruptured when I was 11 and gangrene developed. For 3 days, I went without food and water with a tube down my nose while they drained the infection. Other than that one traumatic incident, I made it until I was 50 years old with plenty of strength and good health. Then in 1993, they removed a herniated disk and 20 bone spurs from my upper neck. My spinal cord ruptured 3 days later and spinal fluid started leaking. For 5 days I lay flat on my back with an irrigation tube draining the fluid from my spine. I developed a staph infection in my spine from the irrigation tube 3 weeks after that. In 1999, I had quadruple bypass surgery following my heart attack. In 2001, they did a total knee replacement on my left knee and the same on my right in 2008. I had 3 rotator cuff surgeries in 2006.

From the time I was a young kid, adults frequently commented on my strength and size. I always felt strong. But when I turned 50, it seemed I started to fall apart. Back pain and arthritis became a part of my everyday life. When I was running headlong into one physical problem after another, it would have been nice to know that the best part of my life was still ahead.

While writing this, I'm past 70. Nowadays, I step back and let the young bulls grab the heavy stuff. When I was young, I never had to back down from anything, but I do now. I look in the mirror, and I don't miss the young guy I used to be. I asked God for a chance with k, held my head high, put on a confident smile, and waited in the coffee shop as a Christian gentleman, not as a young buck. I'm glad that once I decided she was the one I wanted, I didn't let our 8-year age difference or my health issues hold me back.

The Third Time's the Charm?

2 Laces, a Knot, and a Bow!

The way Ron and I met and then married 6 weeks later makes it sound simple, but that's not exactly true. We're amazed at the number of concerts and plays we both attended but never met. Twice a week for 10 years, Ron stocked the convenience store behind my house in Etter. He'd also made deliveries to the office next door to our farm office in Sunray. But the time must not have been right for us to meet – because we didn't.

Though we discussed Betty and John from the day we met, it took a year before we compared the dates. It was spooky the way our life-changing events occurred simultaneously. John died and Betty had her stroke in March of 2006. For 3 years, Ron put aside his regular life to stand by Betty so she could remain at home instead of going to a care facility. During those same 3 years, I hovered in limbo as my strange relationship with my second husband ate up those years of my life. The same week that Ron buried Betty, I buried my youngest son, Adam. For the next 2 years, Ron and I endured all the single life we could stand. After that, with all the countless ways there are for singles to get acquainted, we both went to the exact same website at exactly the same time.

It seems our lives were shoestrings crisscrossing and lacing up the same shoe but never actually meeting until, finally, God brought us together, tied a knot, and made a bow.

Water Hose and Oreo!

The unlucky date we chose was the most memorable thing about our wedding. Because I have a horrible time remembering dates, I thought I could remember Friday the 13th without a problem! Ron had mentioned several times how much he enjoyed sitting in his hot tub beneath the stars. I thought we could get married under the stars in his backyard, just the 2 of us and a preacher, but he wanted to include my children and then like most guest lists, it grew! When the topic of refreshments came up, I suggested a water hose and a package of Oreo cookies, but I had no takers. We wore casual outfits that we already owned. There were no flowers, candles, or chairs. My daughter did sing one verse of "This is the Day" but that was all there was to it. Kenna and the coffee girls took a few snapshots. They're the prettiest pictures I've ever been in. I guess it proves that big smiles and glowing happiness make a bride and a groom of any age more beautiful.

A Honeymoon for 2 Seniors and 4 Little Boys!

More than 6 months before I met k, she promised Jagee and Larry Dan that she would babysit their 4 boys while they went with their church to Israel. The day after the wedding, we drove to Dallas to babysit. That might sound like a lousy honeymoon plan, but it couldn't have been better. After we took the boys to school, we had the day to ourselves. We had very nice accommodations for free. Well, it would have been free, but k invested in the most essential souvenir a newly married couple could want. The very first day, she promised the boys a dollar apiece for each night they went to bed without an argument, didn't fight, or get out of bed.

One very special night, she upped it to 3 bucks each. We couldn't have asked for more privacy. She jokes that she had to cash in her savings bonds to pay us out of hock, but who cares – it was worth every cent!

All or Nothing

From the outset Ron and I have known that our marriage is comprised of 3; God and the 2 of us. Either all 3 of us will be happy or all 3 of us will be disappointed. We are in it together. We believe it makes God happy to see us be good to one another and reverently value what He has entrusted to us.

Before I answered Ron's first email, Ron asked God for a chance to meet me because he thought he could help me. Before we married, I asked God to repay Ron for the 3 years he faithfully stood by Betty and to repay him through me. Each of us selflessly planned to be good to the other. If I were writing a book about the way we met and how incredible our marriage turned out, I would cite those 2 requests as the secrets to the magic. It makes us happy to please one another.

After we were married I told Ron, "No needs, no wants, and no whims will go unmet on my watch!" That's been an easy promise to keep because it's not hard to be good to the one who is so good to me. People frequently say, "I know having the kind of marriage you 2 have must take a lot of work." But cross-my-heart, it is the easiest life I have ever known. All I can say is **Every Day is Sweeter** and easier than the day before; and I wish everyone could live the life we're living and feel the joy we feel.

Unheralded Guidance!

In the Beginning
God Created 4 Perfect Days

We married Friday night, and on Monday morning I told Ron, "These have been the 4 happiest days of my life."

Ron was surprised to hear me say how I felt. It was true. I had never been more fulfilled. For 4 straight days, I had lived completely relaxed and without doubts or inhibitions. I was so happy with Ron, and he made certain that I knew that he was more than satisfied with me. We had no disagreements or disappointments. I had never even seen a frown on his face. It felt as if the windows of heaven had opened up and God was pouring out more blessings than I had room to receive.

I now wonder how differently our marriage might have turned out if instead of talking to Ron, I had kept my mouth shut. What if I had never told him the first 4 days of our marriage had been the 4 happiest days of my life? As soon as I mentioned it, we started paying closer attention to the flawless way things were going and we both wanted it to continue. I couldn't wait to tell the coffee girls about the fantastic way our honeymoon began. Of course, I wished our perfect marriage could last a little longer than 4 days, but we were only human, and there was no way we could keep going without a tiff or a minor irritation. Truthfully, that morning of the fourth day I simply hoped we could make it all the way to midnight without spoiling things. And we did. The next morning, I wondered if we could turn it into the 5 happiest days of my life. I was amazed when it became the happiest week of my life. I went absolutely bonkers when it stretched into the happiest 6 weeks of my life. I couldn't wait to boast about how long we lasted before either one of us got mad. Not once did I think the happiest 4 days of my life could turn into our new way of life.

Classic

When Ron and I married, I expected to enjoy his company when he wasn't watching TV or when we weren't shopping or chatting with family. I guess I thought we would enjoy being friends in our spare time, and I certainly didn't expect him to mark off a big portion of time for his new wife. I didn't think my life would change that much. I'd still run errands for the farm, and he would go to his office. I'd buy groceries, and he'd pay the bills. I'd clean house, and he'd work in the yard. He'd watch sports on TV, and I'd read or make a phone call. I'd constantly complain about him leaving his socks on the floor, and he'd scold me for always making us late. Though Ron and I would sit together in the car, at church, and in restaurants; at home we would both sit in our own recliners. That's the drill, right? We had no expectations of being anything other than a typical married couple.

We assumed our new marriage would take up where we

left off with Betty and John. What else could married life be? This marriage would be a lesser marriage because of our age. We'd had all of our "bright, shiny, new stuff" worn off years ago. It's funny that we could see all the disadvantages we brought to the table and none of the advantages. Ron and I didn't want to marry old people, but after we found one another, all our prejudice went out the window and we headed towards one another at breakneck speed. We didn't think of one another as old, beat-up junkers but as classic '57 Chevys with spinner caps and Laker pipes. In truth, we wanted '57 Chevys when they were brand new but we couldn't afford them. All these years later, we still want them just as much even with all their miles.

Though I cared for Ron and I wanted to be a good wife to him, I didn't give serious thought to getting rid of my old behaviors or bad attitudes. I stopped making New Year's resolutions a long time ago, and I wasn't going to promise myself that I'd be a new and better person after I married. Ron seemed to like me just fine the way I was. I believed his marriage proposal meant "come as you are" and that was exactly what I did. I had every reason to believe my life would remain the way it had always been.

I Never Imagined

What I didn't count on was how different Ron was from anyone I had ever known. He was enthusiastic and upbeat. He complemented me all the time. He was so proud to be seen with me. Wow, what a difference that made. It turned my world upside-down to be treated as if I were beautiful and wonderful. I found myself smiling constantly, and he would say, "There's that beautiful smile I fell in love with." He told me that he liked the sound of my voice and my laughter. I felt foolish and eventually my face started to hurt, but I still couldn't stop smiling and laughing. My emotions and attitudes were being transformed. The new, happier me was full of energy and life and I wanted Ron to feel as incredible as I did and share in the joy he was giving to me. From the outset he started saying, "I love my life." And consequently *I loved my new life as his wife*. We agreed that our marriage turned out to be far more than we bargained for!

Ever since I was a little girl locked inside my front yard, I had wished for a friend. My wish was finally coming true a half-century later when I was 60. Waiting for a lifetime made his arrival even sweeter.

The Secret Ingredient

As soon as I mentioned the 4 happiest days of my life to Ron, I wanted to see them continue, but I didn't know what to attribute our happiness to. One of the major differences between our married life and our single life was the absence of television. Truthfully, if Ron or I had been asked when we were first married if we were willing to go more than a few days without TV we would have said, "NO!"

In the beginning, giving up TV was nothing either of us planned, it just happened. It started the day Ron came to Dumas, and we talked in my driveway. My grandsons had spent the night and hooked their video game up to my TV and after that my television never picked up channels again. Then on our honeymoon, we didn't know how to operate my son-in-law's electronics, so we left their TV alone. When we came home, we immediately moved into our new house and Dish Network put us on a waiting list for service. We went more than 8 weeks without being able to access TV. Of course, we didn't mind at first because we thought it was temporary, and we were pretty much TV-ed out from our years as singles.

We suspected that the absence of television might be a key to our good life. But perfect marriage or no perfect marriage, the question remained *how long could a man be expected to go without watching sports?*

After we bought speakers for our iPod, put them in our bedroom and kitchen, and expanded our music library; we realized that we didn't even need TV for background noise anymore. Ron's interests in sports and mine in HGTV dwindled as Ron worked on the plans for our trip to Scotland, and I worked on writing this book. After more than a year without TV, Ron canceled Netflix.

Ron signed up for the same large package of channels at our new house as he'd always had for Betty. For almost 2 years, we paid to have service to our bedroom and living room without ever watching a single program. Still, Ron just couldn't stand the thought of cancelling. He was convinced, if one of us got sick, we'd be glad we still had Dish.

Since we weren't watching TV, we found one another to be flexible and congenial. We were always willing to step out of our front door and go for a walk around the neighborhood, help one another, and most of all we were willing to talk and to *listen*. Those were the real luxuries we'd been missing while we were single.

Most people can't believe that we don't at least watch the news and weather, but we don't. We hate to admit that because we want you to finish reading our book and you won't if you think we're a couple of kooks! But if you'll just think about it, all families lived without TV until 70 years ago. But today it's considered suspiciously fanatical if a household isn't plugged into everything the media has to offer. Understand, WE ARE NOT RECOMMENDING THE ABANDONMENT OF TELEVISION! But to tell our story without revealing this vital component would be like giving you our prize winning recipe but omitting the most important, secret ingredient.

The main reason we have never returned to TV is so we can give more time and attention to one another. After 2 years, we tried TV one morning and discovered how quickly we could become engrossed in a program and how easy it was to put one another on the back burner. When we saw that we definitely would revert to our old bad habits, it posed 2 simple questions. Did we truly love the way our marriage was? And if so, what were we willing to do to keep it that way?

We're spoiled to 100% of each other's attention and that's the way marriage works best for us; we'll do whatever it takes to hold onto what we have. Someday if we find ourselves bedridden or widowed again, that will be the perfect time for watching TV.

Old Isn't Necessarily "Gold"

The Unexpected Advantages

When we talk about how happily married we are, we don't mean that I'm a better wife than Betty or that Ron's a better husband than John. We're saying that Ron and I are easier to deal with now that we're seniors than when we were younger. There are benefits to getting married at our age. *For the 2 of us, life is easier and so is marriage.*

In our younger years, we struggled to stay in business and raise the kids. It was hard just to survive. But now we're finished, and we welcome a slower pace. We're proud that we stayed the course and made memories with our children. Right now it's just the 2 of us, and we have more free time than ever before. As for those fledgling businesses, they're up and running stronger than ever. I've always known that Justin would grow the farm. I never invested my savings in the stock market. I invested in my people, the farm, and the employees who work hard to make it a success. Ron has the luxury of completely relaxing with Russ at the helm of Mid-West Glove. We can be as involved in the business as we want to be. Life is good. We are undeniably living in the amazing days of whip cream, sprinkles, and a cherry on top.

They say, "The richest person isn't the one who has the most but the one who needs the least." When we were young married people, we wanted everything because we started out with nothing. Back then, we chased all the shiny new stuff. As seniors we drive by garbage dumps and realize that rusty old junk was the cause of many an argument back in the day. We've finally figured out that the atmosphere is more important than the stuff. We're happy with less, and we're enjoying it more.

We don't over commit to outside interests. When we were lonely, we weren't selective about the things that filled our lives. We would sign up or agree to anything because all that mattered was staying busy. It feels strange to turn down invitations now, but occasionally we do. We enjoy simply being together. I help out in his office, he goes with me on farm errands, and the work around the house we do together.

The greatest senior advantage is that we've learned from all the mistakes we've made. We listen and value one another's opinion. We never say, "The discussion is over!" We don't complain about one another to other people. We're loyal.

Ron thinks I'm a nice person, and he wishes we could have married when we were young and had our children together. Well, he's not so wrong. I am fairly nice now! But I had to have a lot of mean rubbed off of me before I became this way. I've been in a marriage where I was offended and one where I was selfish. I know all the verses to both those songs. I've changed many of my wrong attitudes and every change I've made has produced this nicer wife that Ron's enjoying.

More than anything, Ron and I bring out the best in one another.

When Ron prayed and said that he could love me if God would give him the chance, he was on the right track. His love has made a world of difference. And I meant it when I said, "No needs, no wants, no whims will go unmet on my watch." God is doing great things in my life through this husband. I owe them both! I find being more pleasant and agreeable is starting to become more natural. Every day is easier than the day before. No longer am I trying to hang on to our perfect record just so I can brag to my friends.

Nothing has helped us take our relationship seriously more than the death of Betty and John. We know lots of people live to be much older than we are but a lot of people don't. We realize that death is on a conveyer belt, and it's constantly moving toward us. We're not troubled that we may have only a short time together; we're motivated. This is our last lap. With both of us widowed and divorced, we would be fools to mess this up. Living single for years, we became accustom to peace but not silence. We didn't marry so we'd have a spouse to argue with, be critical of, or give the silent treatment to. That was our unspoken agreement when we married. What we didn't know was how easy it would be to live this peaceful, happy way. Our discovery came as a *gradual revelation* after the first 4 days of marriage. *Since God gave us that BIG push off, we have kept right on pedaling and never looked back!*

Intimacy is Knowing 😊

k and I feel we've known each other forever. We didn't know how close we would quickly become just by sharing our life stories. Betty didn't want to reveal her past so she never questioned me about mine. But k's an interested listener, always asking for further explanation and more details. It's flattering when she asks me to repeat one of my stories for her grandchildren. I trust her with everything. Consequently, she knows me better than my sisters and understands me better than Taylor. We live without walls or locks.

Words Are Cheap 😊

Early in our relationship, k said she was approachable and teachable but later she changed her wording to, "*I want to be ap-*

proachable and teachable." I felt it was from her heart. But over the years, I had salesmen make boasts in their interview that never proved true after I hired them. My mom always cautioned me that the proof was in the pudding. So even though it was a nice claim to be approachable and teachable, I intended to keep an eye on her because time would tell.

k first demonstrated her approachability soon after we married. We sometimes ate on our loveseat. Since the only time k held Okly was when she sat on the loveseat, Oak sat at attention right by her feet from the moment we sat down. Okly was waiting for the pat on k's lap that would be her invitation to join us. If k finished eating before I did, she'd let Okly hop up on her lap. I didn't like the back end or front end of Okly so close to my food while I was still eating. After a couple of times, I told her that I didn't enjoy her dog sitting eye level with my food while I finished my meal.

I was aware that I might have just lit k's fuse. I knew people who would never come right out and say their dog was more important to them than people, when actually, that's the way it was. Okly was my big concern from the first time I saw k holding the little white fluff ball in her CM pictures. I'd never lived with a dog in my house. I knew Okly might be a problem after we married. I wondered if push ever came to shove what value k put on my preferences when it came to her dog. Much to my surprise, k accepted it pleasantly and never again allowed Okly up until I was finished eating. Because k never forgot that Oak was the dog and I was the husband, it made it easy for me to enjoy having Okly around.

Not long after we were married, k asked me if her driving instructions were irritating me. When I said, "YES!" she said, "I was afraid of that. I'm going to stop saying anything even if I have to ride with my eyes closed." I thought, *Hey girl, your life is still in my hands whether your eyes are closed or not but go ahead if you think that will help.* Sure enough, that's exactly what she did – she would close her eyes as we approached a red light or a turning lane until eventually she got out of the habit of giving me driving tips. Okly and k's driving tips were the first 2 instances that I recall k proving that she really was approachable and teachable, as she aimed to be.

I interpreted teachable as doing whatever it took to get along. I liked the little expressions she used, "team player" and "get on board," when we talked about functioning together without getting irritated. Daily I was amazed as she proved her willingness to do whatever it took to please me and frequently told me, "I want what you want." That made me feel honored, and it ignited a desire within me to love her back in all the same ways.

The No-Brainer

Before I ever met Ron, I realized that I had been a grumpy, old fuddy-duddy from my early years. I adamantly believed that all my opinions were right, and everyone should want to hear them and joyfully accept them. I suppose that's who I'll always be at my core even though I fight it. It is a constant struggle, but I must reel it in or die alone.

I remind myself that Ron has driven since he was 14 and somehow managed to survive without a backseat driver. I have a choice. I can stop trying to control his driving and enjoy a pleasant ride, or I can ruin everything. It's a no-brainer.

Introduced to An angel

Once on a long trip, she said she'd like to pull over and show me something. The first thing that came to my mind was, *k always tells me that she wants what I want, and this is my opportunity to do the same for her.* How ridiculous it would have been for me to put her off with, "Maybe another time, but not now. We're in a hurry." Of all things, she wanted to stop at a cemetery and show me a headstone. She promised it was unlike anything I had ever seen. The last thing I would have thought of doing on a long trip would have been to visit a cemetery. But I'm glad we stopped because otherwise I would have missed the opportunity to make my wife happy, and making k happy is important to me. We walked and read headstones for practically an hour. She showed me the headstone that she said was her very favorite. It wasn't a picture of an angel but actually a sculpture of an angel with flowers leaning over the headstone weeping. As k pointed out all that the statue meant to her, I came to know my wife a little better, and by stopping, k came to see that even her small requests are important to me.

Getting Out-of-Town

Scooch a Little Closer, Darling

Sharing the same financial values and attitudes made life even easier. We had never lived extravagant lives because the lean years in our past had left their indelible marks on us. We were careful with our pennies, and we enjoyed knowing we could afford to live out a couple of our dreams even though we thought we never would. We listened to people talk about their vacations and it always sounded wonderful, but we didn't have anyone to accompany us and since we didn't want to go alone it was obvious that we were never going. For years our dreams were neatly folded and tucked away. It took us getting married before we bought our tickets, packed our bags, and ran out the door on our way.

After we married, Ron took me to New York City for my sixty-first birthday, and I took him to Scotland for his seventieth. We've also gone to the Biltmore and on an Alaskan cruise. On our trips, we saw plenty of folks who were traveling alone, and they seemed to be comfortable and enjoying themselves, but it just made the 2 of us scooch a little closer together.

Each trip has been like a dream come true. We always have a fantastic time. It hasn't been seeing the sights that made it great, but having an awesome friend to enjoy them with. My definition of an awesome friend is a trooper - someone who carries on and doesn't blame or complain when there's a problem. We earned our trooper badges the day we traveled from Dublin to Paris. First, we flew from Dublin to London. Then, we took the underground tube from the airport to catch the Eurostar train for Paris. When we got off the subway, we could see feet walking on ground level from where we stood at the bottom of the escalator. That's how close we were. All we had to do was get up to the street and cross to the train station!

We had 4 pieces of luggage on wheels. Ron headed to the escalator, and I called to him that the elevator was right there behind us. We were already at the foot of the escalator, but to get to the elevator we would have to cross through the crowd of moving pedestrians. Ron opted for us to simply step on the escalator and ride it up to the street. That sounded simple enough. We both put one of our suitcases on the step in front of us and the other one on the step behind us. Halfway up our largest bag, which was in front of Ron, pitched back towards him, and he let go of the handrail to catch it. Without holding to the handrail, the weight of the suitcase threw him off balance, and he fell backwards. He twisted so he would land on his stomach and onto the bag behind him. It fell into my front suitcase, and it knocked me down. I twisted as I fell onto my bag behind me. Undoubtedly we looked like dominoes falling. We were both on our stomachs, with our feet above our heads, while we slid down on top of suitcases. We would never have reached the bottom because the escalator steps were constantly rising, and we were continually sliding down. Thank God, someone hit the emergency button and it eventually stopped!

Evidently the nervous first aid lady had never had an emergency before. She panicked at the sight of our blood and was totally useless. She repeatedly insisted, "We must call an ambulance. You need stitches!" When she took us to her first aid room, it was actually a janitor's closet. She couldn't get her latex gloves on and the empty glove tips dangled off the ends of her fingers as she tried to work. Exasperated, she finally jerked them off. She jabbed her car keys into the cellophane wrapper on the gauze strips to get them opened. We realized we would miss our train if we didn't take matters into our own hands. So we both washed the blood off our wounds in the mop sink beneath the posted warning sign that said the water wasn't fit for human consumption. They warned us about the rats that lived beneath the escalator and the serious need for tetanus shots unless we had recently had them.

We limped away, took the train to Paris, got out in the pouring rain, and stood in line for 2 hours for a taxi. When it was finally our turn for a taxi, the first one turned us down because we had too much luggage, the second taxi driver got lost and our short ride cost us 25 euros. We walked to a 24-hour pharmacy that wouldn't sell us hydrogen peroxide and fresh bandages without a prescription. Paris had no urgent care facility so the hotel called a doctor who came to our room in the middle of the night. He wrote prescriptions for bandages and sterile wash. He gave us no stitches, shots, or medicines and it cost us 175 euros! Again, we walked back to the pharmacy. They didn't have everything to fill our pre-scriptions so they told us to return the next morning. On our way back to the hotel, we were confused, made a wrong turn, and walked forever. As if that were not enough – it started to rain! The next morning we missed our prepaid small group tour of the Eiffel Tower because we were getting tetanus shots, shots that Dr. Whelchel urged us to take when we saw him the week before our trip, but I turned him down.

Believe it or not, there was much more that went wrong, but I think you get the general idea. That proved to be sufficient for Ron and me to earn our trooper badges! Ron never mentioned that we wouldn't have missed our Eiffel Tower tour if I hadn't refused the tetanus shots, and I never mentioned that we could have taken the elevator and skipped the entire incident. We're not saints. We're experienced! We've learned that the vacation winds up being a few photographs and a funny story about almost dying on an escalator. We didn't get mad at one another even when we were trudging along all bruised and sore the night we were lost in downtown Paris while it rained. We attribute it to maturity.

We'd rather sit on our patio wearing t-shirts and flip flops and eating fried wiener sandwiches together than eat alone in the fanciest French restaurant in Paris. Even the mundane task of refilling our pill organizers is pleasant because we're together.

Ron and I found in one another an adventurer for the extraordinary times and a buddy for the ordinary days. Someone we will passionately kiss goodnight forever.

Physical

Friends Encourage Friends

After we got married, k's girlfriend got involved with an unscrupulous man. I told k why I suspected the guy wasn't to be trusted. Her friend believed in him, and k was torn between my opinion of the man and her friend's. As the situation progressed, k began to have her own doubts. She became frantic that her friend was about to be taken advantage of by a lowlife. I had to warn her several times that she was becoming too involved, and she needed to back off and let it go. She would agree with me, but in no time she'd be right back in there pleading with her friend to take it slow and not to give in because we were sure she would regret it.

One night I told her, "I never had a friend like you who encouraged me to make the right moral decisions."

She gave me a big smile and said, "Oh yes you did."

I said, "Really, who?"

She said, "Me! I was there for you just like I'm here for her."

I'd never looked at it that way. I never thought of her as a friend who was encouraging me to do the right thing when she said we weren't going to get physical. I agreed to it, but even back then I thought it was overkill. Since we've been married, every time this subject comes up, I stand my ground that it didn't have to be so extreme. I was a mature, Christian man not a teenage boy. I wasn't going to let my hormones get out of control. All I wanted was to pull her close and hug her or give her a little goodnight kiss. But k said she had enough to do just keeping her own passions suppressed without having to fight mine as well. So, I dropped the subject for 2 reasons. I didn't want to argue, and my track record wasn't exactly a shining example of self-control.

Don't Jump the Gun

We have a very real sense of the presence of God. We're amazed at what he planned for us. I wonder if I would have disqualified myself from this girl-next-door if I'd gone home with the woman from the gym. k's certain she would have disqualified herself after her divorce if she'd remained bitter and punished herself by re-treating from life to sit quietly on a shelf and feel guilty.

All our talk about waiting and doing things God's way certainly wasn't our original idea. When we were at lunch with my high school grandson, Matthew, k asked him about the ring he was wearing. He said it symbolized his commitment to remain pure and save himself for his wife. I thought, *How awesome it must be to realize the value of purity at a young age.* I know it will be hard. I pray for him to be strong enough to live up to his commitment and experience the payoff for such a sacrifice. It's amazing that there are so many adults who consider themselves Godly people of integrity, including church leaders, who also consider virginity and celibacy to be old-fashioned ideas or romantic notions that grownups tell children and younger teenagers.

No Deal-Breaker

I remember that even before Betty's health became the main issue, I was having symptoms that caused me concern. My urolo-gist assured me that he had a buddy who was a doctor in Las Ve-gas; he could fix me right up if all else failed. I didn't like the sound of that. All concerns about sex were shelved as Betty's health continually declined even to the point of hospice. More than 7 years later when k came into my life, I had no idea what I might have left. We discussed everything the day we set our wedding date and decided since both of us had already been living celibate lives for many years, if that never changed, we could still have a wonderful life together as husband and wife.

I'm glad that before we married we never allowed that unsolved problem to become a deal-breaker. We married for something much greater than sex, and going ahead with the marriage without knowing what the future held proved that we meant what we said. We started out as supportive friends, and we have continued. We face whatever the future holds together.

Make God Proud

We were seniors who'd been married more than half our lives to other people. We both had habits and hang-ups from our past that could have been obstacles and made for bad sex. Not to mention creaking, older bodies. Instead, in the first 5 minutes our pasts became nonexistent, and we were swarmed by endorphins!

God was not only my source when I first thought of finding a lady to date; He is our partner as a married couple. He made old things become brand new. k and I want everyone to know about the awesome thing God has done for us and continues to do. We have discussed it and decided it's probably best to merely encourage couples to make their romantic and physical relationships one that God would be proud to be a part of. Before long, the tables will turn, and God will make the marriage one that you will be proud to be a part of.

Just remember to please the one you love and make sure the

one you love isn't yourself.

No Longer a Problem

Today we can look at the good and bad events from before and see where they have all been stepping-stones to this good place. Some past problems are no longer problems, but we didn't find that out until after we married. Let's just say that *some things can be corrected.*

Science has put a man on the moon, in case you haven't heard; medically they have more than pills to help seniors. My old urologist had retired, and I took an appointment with an indifferent younger doctor. I suppose that punk could have been the end of the trail for me. Thank God my name was in the system at the Amarillo Urology Center, and I got one of their mail outs inviting me to Dr. Kibbey's seminar at BSA hospital. The most unbelievable part was that Medicare covered 95% of the expense. That's probably because our congress, who decides how best to spend our tax dollars, is comprised of men who are looking out for their own futures.

Any problem that can't be corrected doesn't have to be a dead end. k and I truly love one another. We have open communication. We stand together as a team when we have an issue. We don't disband or turn against one another. Even if we can't get a victory, we don't allow the problem to separate us.

My Sister Threatened to Boycott My Book If I Talked about Sex!

Thousands & Thousands

Until I married Ron, my life was always in a hurry. I never knew a husband and wife could wake up in the morning and linger in bed talking. It's so wonderful not to be alone. I look at the man who loves me lying on the pillow next to mine, and I thank God. Some mornings I just stare at him in disbelief. How could my life have come so far? Who would have thought it could happen to me? Other mornings he wakes up first and he's staring at me. I scooch over and put my head on his shoulder. I like to rub his arm while we talk. If we remember our dreams, we share them. We say how we are feeling or how we slept. Sometimes we go over the plans for the day, if we have any. On the weekends we drink coffee in bed. We sit and read aloud, and afterwards we discuss what we read. Sometimes, we just reminisce.

We're not young. We snore. Bed head is not stylish for seniors, but it can't be avoided. When I was young, I worried about that stuff, but not anymore. We have prayed and waited for someone to love for so long that we don't let little stuff get in the way. After all, each of us is the answer to the other's prayers and that makes us miracles!

Gone are those mornings when I stayed in bed because I was too depressed to make myself get up; when my spare time was a burden, and I worked just to stay busy. Instead of filling time we set aside time to enjoy the thing *God prepared exclusively for a husband and wife.* We enjoy allowing romance and intimacy to simmer until it's perfect. We're in no rush. A physical relationship has been missing for THOUSANDS of mornings and THOUSANDS of nights for both of us. That's a long time to go without so much as a kiss. And there was no indication that a change would ever come our way.

Unless we're in a car wreck and die together, one of us is destined to be left alone *again* someday. We want no regrets because we omitted pleasing one another.

I love Ronald with all my heart, and there is nothing I wouldn't do for him. I might not want to get up and get my own Tylenol, but I'll hop out of bed to run get one for him. I would give him my kidney if he needed one. A Tylenol and a kidney are nice gestures. But in reality Ron would prefer "*Something Else*" as the token of my love…and so would I!

The bride in Song of Solomon said it for both of us, "He is my beloved, my lover, and my friend. And I am his."

The Benefit of Experience

My Expensive Life Lessons!

I got one thing I've always wanted in my divorce – I got to change my name. I dropped my first name, Virgie, and changed the spelling of Kay to k – a single, lowercase letter. That was the one good thing.

I did learn many things from my divorce that I had not understood previously. I learned that even though I had a wedding, I didn't have a marriage. I also learned that I was as divorced as a woman could be even while I was still legally married. And I learned that after something is dead, it's too late to start mouth-to-mouth resuscitation.

Through the 3 years of that relationship, I experienced passive aggression, unresolved anger, frustration, failure, regret, and guilt. I've thought about the entire experience from beginning to end. I have worried myself sick and beaten myself up, and it changed absolutely nothing. Well, at least it changed nothing with my second marriage. It did make unbelievable changes in me. It allowed me to recognize many of my mistakes, and I don't intend to repeat them with Ronald.

In my second marriage, we married because we hated being alone. I learned that there is something much worse than sitting at a dinner table alone, riding in a vehicle alone, and lying in bed alone. That's sitting, riding, and lying beside someone in total silence and deliberately never touching. Our marriage could easily be summed up in one word…withholding.

I also learned something valuable from my 36 years with John. He and I loved one another from the beginning, and we never stopped loving one another, but we allowed the luster and the sparks to fade. The Righteous Brothers sing "You've lost that loving feeling" about the thrill of new love being dulled by disappointment as sweethearts take one another for granted. When those first feelings of being madly in love with the perfect person are gone, you can get down on your knees and beg but you can't get them back and neither can your spouse. John and I were young and we didn't realize what we had. Quickly, we discarded our honeymoon phase. We were anxious to begin life as married adults, always in a hurry, and with lots to do. That was the way our sparks faded.

Sometimes I feel guilty that John and I lost our *initial* loving feelings while Ron and I have been able to maintain them. I doubt John and I could have ever gotten them back. Ron says if Betty and John had been the survivors instead of us and they had found others to marry, they would have had the **maturity** to *cherish and preserve* a new marriage. And that makes me feel better because *I know it's true.*

Well, This is the End of the Line

We hope you enjoyed our book and you feel that we are friends. Squeezing both of our lives into 149 pages was a tight fit. We had so many memories to choose from but we finally settled on the ones that revealed the most.

This book is the story of ordinary us being guided to the thing we wanted most. God kept His plan a secret but once the blindfolds came off, we had everything we had longed for.

The original reason we told our story was for our nieces, nephews, and grandchildren to know the truth. We want them to be aware that we were once impressionable children and to know about the ups and downs of our adult lives. We have an amazing marriage now, but it was God's doing, not ours. We hope our story will give them comfort and confidence that beyond the darkest times there can still be good days ahead.

Not every widowed or divorced person is unhappy. Some widowers are looking for guys who meet for breakfast and discuss sports, hunting, and fishing. Some widows are looking for girlfriends to join them for lunch, shopping, and bunko. Our book is not intended to stimulate dissatisfaction or unrest in single people who are alone but not lonely. Different people want different things out of life. If you are one of those well-satisfied singles, you are where we all want to be. Thank you for taking the time to thumb through our little book.

But for some of you, a late-in-life romantic interest or marriage could make all the difference and

we have shared our story to encourage you!